Life Keeps Me Dancing

Life Keeps Me Dancing

Eileen Kramer

Pan Macmillan Australia

Pan Macmillan acknowledges the Traditional Custodians of Country throughout Australia and their connections to lands, waters and communities. We pay our respect to Elders past and present and extend that respect to all Aboriginal and Torres Strait Islander peoples today. We honour more than sixty thousand years of storytelling, art and culture.

First published 2023 in Macmillan by Pan Macmillan Australia Pty Ltd
1 Market Street, Sydney, New South Wales, Australia, 2000

Copyright © Eileen Kramer 2023

The moral right of the author to be identified as the author of this work has been asserted.

All rights reserved. No part of this book may be reproduced or transmitted by any person or entity (including Google, Amazon or similar organisations), in any form or by any means, electronic or mechanical, including photocopying, recording, scanning or by any information storage and retrieval system, without prior permission in writing from the publisher.

A catalogue record for this book is available from the National Library of Australia

Typeset in 12.5/18 Adobe Garamond Pro by Midland Typesetters, Australia

Printed by IVE

The author and the publisher have made every effort to contact copyright holders for material used in this book. Any person or organisation that may have been overlooked should contact the publisher.

The paper in this book is FSC® certified. FSC® promotes environmentally responsible, socially beneficial and economically viable management of the world's forests.

For my mother and father

Contents

Chapter One	Sydney / Basic Shapes	1
Chapter Two	Phillip Street / Intellectual Passions	17
Chapter Three	Meeting Madame / The Ecstasy of Purpose	35
Chapter Four	Life Class / Art and Dance	55
Chapter Five	Australian Tours / In Good Company	69
Chapter Six	Gateway to India / Colour and Movement	89
Chapter Seven	Bombay / The Big Picture	105
Chapter Eight	No Fixed Abode / India Bag	121
Chapter Nine	Paris / A Frozen Dancer	137
Chapter Ten	New York / Stop Motion	155
Chapter Eleven	West Virginia / Just You Wait	183
Chapter Twelve	Sydney / Let's Dance	205
Acknowledgements		223

'To dance is to take part in the cosmic control of the world.'
– Havelock Ellis, 'The Philosophy of Dancing', *The Atlantic*, 1914

Chapter One

Sydney / Basic Shapes

THE BODY HAS ITS MEMORIES. THOSE MEMORIES hold strong, even when the body changes.

I have a lovely mirror, now; I often sit before it and dance as I sift through the memories this body carries.

Mirrors have always been important to me. As a little girl I would stand in front of them for hours, changing my shape, holding poses, taking up space. I see that little girl in my reflection now. Then I see myself as a young woman.

I flow from one position to another. Left hand, right hand, following the movement of my arm, shoulder, breath. Reaching out. Feeling the resistance of the air. Then back again.

It's organic; I do not switch from one firm position to another. There are no firm positions here, but, as in life, there is a continuous shifting, like a cloud that keeps changing shape.

I can dance in the mirror for hours. Not out of vanity, but out of love.

Until recently, I've always felt that everyone was older than me. That everyone around me was an adult, and I was still on my way. These days, when I look into my lovely mirror, I suppose I am finally all grown up.

My name is Eileen Kramer. I am a dancer. I've been dancing for more than one hundred years, and I like to think I'm getting the hang of it. I am not old. I've just been here a long time. I was born at home in Paddington, Sydney, in the evening of 8 November 1914, and that's all I ever like to say about my age. I don't remember Paddington; my first memories are of Mosman, on the northern shore of the harbour, where I grew up.

Sydney was a very different place at that time. The city was young, with all the excitement and joy and foolishness of youth. Although the people of the First Nations had lived, danced and sung on this land for thousands and thousands of years, Sydney itself was just over one hundred and twenty years old. All the grand sandstone buildings, the red-roofed cottages against the glittering blue of the water – all new. New too were the Europeans and other migrants who had travelled from overseas to make a home.

My mother was Hilda Henrietta. Her family came to Australia from England. My father, Julius Kramer, was born in South Africa, but his family had come from Germany. That's where I get my name: Eileen Kramer. I was a little girl in Sydney, a city that was in many ways a child as well – for a while, we grew up together, gazing out over the ocean.

I suppose we have both changed a great deal in that time, but some things never do. The skyscrapers have gone up, and Bondi Beach is now famous around the world, but there are over a hundred bays and beaches along the Sydney shoreline, and the small, secret shoals and islands I knew in childhood look almost the same today.

I grew up exploring the coast with my father, who loved to sail. He owned a boat named the *Astoria*, which he moored near where we lived in Mosman Bay. It had two cabins, a tiny bathroom and a galley kitchen with a long table where we had our meals. There was also a sort of lounge area in the stern of the boat, large enough for whole families to relax. My father would steer the boat with a little help from my brother, Edward, who was eighteen months older than me. He managed quite well, which was no small feat, given the size of the vessel.

In the afternoon we'd put down the anchor in some nice, sheltered cove and we'd take the dinghy to shore for a picnic. If there was a nice, sandy shore, we'd go swimming before heading below deck and falling asleep to the sound of waves lapping against the hull. We'd wake to the cry of seagulls, and the wonderful laugh of the kookaburra. In my memory, the kookaburra's laugh will always live in that first quiet of the morning, somewhere near the dreams it pulled me from.

A day by the water is never wasted, even when all you do is play. Especially so, perhaps. When my mother wasn't tidying in the cabins or preparing meals, she liked to sit there and gaze dreamily at the sea. Now and again she'd exclaim when she caught sight of a school of dolphins frolicking out in the waves. Stare long enough at the ocean and you never know what you will see – dolphins, flying fish, perhaps even a whale. There is little more fascinating than watching the waves and dreaming of what might lie beneath.

In recent years, people seem to have fallen into the habit of asking me where creativity comes from. I wish they wouldn't. To be quite honest, I don't have the answer for them. All I can say is that the more attention you pay to life, the more interesting it becomes.

I remember being a little girl, bent over some cloth, concentrating on it intently. It was a perfectly ordinary stretch of plain cotton, but I distinctly recall scrutinising the blank surface, and finding in it the shape of a dress. There, clear as day, I could discern the basic shape of a dress for my doll. It was as simple as cutting it out, double-wide, and making a hole for my doll to put her head through and another two for her arms. The result was a very crude sort of a dress, but it was important to me.

I recall this so vividly because, some time later, a neighbour asked me about my doll's new outfit: 'Why is she wearing her nightgown?'

What a silly woman, I thought to myself. It was quite clear that this was a dress.

At the time, it didn't seem like such a noteworthy thing to have dressed my doll up – the shape of the dress was there already, just waiting to be noticed. But when I look back now, I can see this was my first genuine creation. Something that one day didn't exist, and then it did. Even though I was so young, I think I recognised this, and I've never forgotten the feeling.

To me, dance, costume-making, writing, drawing all go together. I suspect I am still like I was when I was a child and I made my first doll's dress. Basically, I haven't changed very much. But that's alright; as Picasso says, we have to learn to paint like children.

A love of learning has always been part of my nature. I can trace this back to one of my earliest memories, from when I was just four or five years old. I was sitting on the kitchen step with a book and pencil in my lap, looking out over the lawn, when I suddenly cried out: 'Mummy!'

The cry was so urgent that my mother dropped everything and rushed straight to my side. I looked up and told her that I had discovered the most fabulous thing – how to spell 'egg'. Mother responded with what might be considered my first generous review – wondering out loud how she had ever come to give birth to such a child genius. She encouraged me to keep learning, and suggested I learn how to spell 'ham' which went wonderfully with 'egg'.

As the years passed, I began to take an interest in things of a scientific nature. All the mysteries of life and death fascinated me. At around seven years old, a friend of the family came to visit, and helped me bury a dead bee in a matchbox in the garden. I planned to dig it up in a few years to find out whether it had turned to dust. My experiment failed when I grew impatient and dug it up after only a few months, finding it more or less unchanged. Disappointed, I turned my field of research to the living, and spent hours watching tadpoles in the back gully lose their tails and grow into frogs. I could not imagine anything more wondrous than the tadpole – a perfect little creature on its own, but with the most incredible destiny inside it. I wondered then if the tadpole understood the journey it would go on, the promise it held. I wondered if it understood how beautiful it was. It's something I still ponder.

My mother encouraged me and told my father that I was a thoughtful child who might one day become a scientist. That was not to be. Apparently, I too had a destiny waiting for me. A fortune-teller at a friend's birthday party told me that I was destined to become a singer. In retrospect, I can't vouch for the provenance of the fortune-teller or think of a reason for a genuine mystic to be at a child's birthday party in Sydney, but one takes their cues where one finds them, so I set my sights on the stage.

At the age of nine or ten, I staged my first theatrical production. The venue was the back veranda of the house. The company of players: my brother and several schoolfriends. There were two items on the bill. The first was 'Bluebeard: A Drama in One Act'. With a set design and special-effects budget limited to what we could find around the house, I had to improvise.

To properly set the gory scene where Bluebeard's young wife enters his hidden dungeon and finds the heads of his previous wives, I hung a white sheet up across the veranda and cut slits at various heights for our actors to poke their heads through. Their hair was then gathered up into ponytails and hooked onto the front of the sheet, so that it gave the effect of decapitated heads hanging from hooks against a white wall. My brother played Bluebeard, and I was the one wife who escaped his wrath. Afterwards, I danced an improvised 'Dance of the Veils' with a gauze cloth that I drew over my eyes.

Thrilled by the success of my concert, I told my mother that I was destined for the stage when I grew up. She was less enthusiastic about this idea than the life of science she'd imagined, and seemed to find the idea of a young woman on stage unseemly. So after that, I kept my longing for the stage to myself, and eventually stopped thinking about it. After a while I began to think that perhaps I would be an artist, and took up drawing pictures of film stars instead – which pleased my mother no end.

As a young girl, I was happy to play, to dabble, to try new things. It was a very good life, exploring the coast, going for long drives in the country. At a time when few families had cars, my father worked in the motor car business, and was able to take us on the most wonderful journeys in an Oldsmobile with a great, clattering, smoky engine. The most exciting thing about those trips for us children were the stories he would tell us about driving through Africa for the Hupmobile company, and all the wild sights he had seen, the people he had met. Big game hunters and pygmies and all sorts of natural wonders. The excitement of what he described always made me want to see the world.

My mother was very beautiful. Her hair enchanted me; long and golden, she wore it pinned up during the day. At night when she went to bed, she would take each hairpin out, laying them down on her dresser with a neat tap. She'd carefully comb her hair, part it at the back, and twist each side into thick braided ropes to frame her face. She looked to me like a Nordic princess. In the mornings, I would go to my parents' bedroom, and she would let me unwind them while my father watched from his pillow.

One day she went to the hairdresser and had her hair cut short. That evening, when my father came home, he changed his seat at the dinner table so that he could look out the window instead of at her. For three days he refused to look at her at all.

Our life fell apart the way that lives often do: gradually, then suddenly. My father drank. A little at first, but then a lot.

Julius Kramer was not a bad man. Not evil, or violent, or neglectful. He committed no grave sins; as far as we knew he'd never been with another woman. He simply drank. He'd stay alone in his room, night after night, drinking more than any man should. At heart, he was a loving father and good husband, but the demon drink consumed him.

As he became worse, our mother became more worried and angry. She would scold him – too much, I thought. It was clear the drink had a grip on him that no amount of nagging would help. It was a helpless situation, for which she was desperate for a solution.

The tension – my father retreating further into the drink, my mother admonishing him for something he seemed to have no control over – caused me to withdraw from both of them. This went on for two years, until one day, when I was thirteen, some removal men turned up and, under our mother's watchful eye, packed up some of our furniture and belongings. She had decided to move us children and our cat, Normie, to a new home – a small cottage in a beach suburb called Coogee, on the other side of Sydney. I would not see my father for a very long time.

The divorce meant a great change for us, and a new school for me. I didn't like it at all, and felt I wasn't learning anything. So one day I simply left and never went back. My poor mother didn't object. She was still reeling from the breakup of her marriage, and hardly seemed to know what was going on. She went to work to support us, working as a store detective, vigilant against shoplifting, while I went about growing up.

In 1933, at the age of nineteen, I took singing and piano lessons from a local teacher. I could sing quite well, but to do so in public made me nervous. Nonetheless, I decided I would like to study seriously at the Conservatorium of Music on Macquarie Street in Sydney. My mother happily agreed to this, as she'd been worried about what would become of me without a proper education. I don't know whether she really believed that I would one day sing opera, but she was pleased that, in the spring of 1935, I became a voice student in classical music at the Conservatorium.

I don't think she ever truly believed I would be able to look after myself. To her, I gave off an air of helplessness, which I considered to be an air of independence.

Practically, this meant I simply rejected anything I didn't want, even if I hadn't quite worked out what it was I *did* want.

Around the time I began studying music, my mother got married again – to a man with seven children who lived out in the suburbs in Hurstville. It was clear I would have to find my own place to live.

With the help of our landlady, Mrs Shlink, I responded to a notice in the newspaper and together we went to see a room in the city available for lease.

As the daughter of a hotel proprietor, Mrs Shlink was somehow drawn to such unconventional living situations, and I was glad of it.

We took the tramcar from Coogee and got off at the square with Queen Victoria's statue; I thought she looked as though she were controlling the traffic around her. Mrs Shlink and I walked a little way along Macquarie Street. This was all new to me, and I marvelled at the wonderful buildings. As we turned into Phillip Street the buildings became less marvellous. There were a few houses that looked as if they had been grand homes of important people once upon a time. Now they wore their years, along with cardboard notices, mostly hanging from windowsills, with the words 'Room to Let'.

I saw one that stirred romantic feelings in me and hoped this was the place we were coming to see. Mrs Shlink, however, walked straight past that one, and stopped before the doorway of a simple white cottage that didn't look grand at all.

She did not enter right away but prowled about for a while as if getting the vibrations of the place. At last, she opened a small wooden gate at the side of the house and led me through a passage into the most delightful courtyard. A weeping willow lent its shade to the centre of the yard, and beneath it sheltered a sort of fairy-tale summerhouse. At least, that's how it looked to my eyes. In the end it turned out to be a lavatory.

As we stood looking at the courtyard with a certain amount of awe, the side door of the white cottage opened and a thin little lady with spiky white hair emerged.

'Have you come about the room?' she asked. When Mrs Shlink confirmed we had indeed, the lady said, 'I'm Mrs Henderson, the landlady here. Follow me, please.' She led us up the rickety wooden stairs to a long balcony on the second floor. Extracting a key from somewhere on her person, she opened a door and invited us to enter the room.

While Mrs Shlink and Mrs Henderson discussed terms and rules, I looked out over the balcony and saw a girl about my age crossing the courtyard, dragging a large, stretched canvas behind her. I was excited by the thought of living here. The girl with the canvas looked interesting. Maybe she would be my friend?

The two older women came to an agreement about the rent and then turned to me: 'Do you like it?'

'I love it,' I said. Truly I did. I'd dreamt of finding a perfect palace, with a grand piano in one corner and a Spanish shawl draped over a table in another. However, the moment I saw this room off the Phillip Street Courtyard, that dream evaporated in the soft, clean sunlight. This room was mine, as if it had been waiting for me all this time. A week later, in March of 1936, I moved in.

Chapter Two

Phillip Street / Intellectual Passions

The girl dragging her canvas across the courtyard to her room under the stairs was Rosaleen Norton – or 'Roie' to her friends, which I soon counted myself among.

Roie was the sweetest of young women, kind, with a middle-class respectability that belied the reputation she would later acquire. She would invite me over for tea with the air of a refined hostess, despite our humble living situation.

'Would you like some tea?' she would ask, in a posh tone, before presenting plain black tea in a mug that could have used a wash.

I didn't mind, because Roie was such a lovely person. She had an easy smile, which would light up her whole face.

I could have sat in her room and talked for hours, but I found her art somewhat disquieting. She was a serious painter, dear Roie, and ferociously talented, although I must say her work was not to my taste. She was obsessed with demons, monsters and horned creatures with glaring eyes and gaping mouths, all things horrific. While I admired her skill, I could not bring myself to appreciate her quite medieval style. I would sit uneasily among the demons adorning every wall, while Roie and I drank tea and chatted.

One of her funniest paintings was called *The Vicar's Picnic*. It featured a vicar seated with assorted ladies and gentlemen around a picnic blanket. Their day had been ruined by a naked nymph charging out of the bushes, followed by a faun, who raced straight through the picnic and knocked the vicar and everybody about. I could see why more conservative elements of society may not have approved.

Later in life, Roie would become quite celebrated as a painter, as well as the notorious 'Witch of Kings Cross'. All sorts of rumours have floated around about her, which I could never quite reconcile with the sweet girl I knew.

She did paint her eyebrows so that they lifted up at the corner, and swept her hair back from her forehead, so she had a witch-like look about her. Not to mention the tiny witch's brooch she wore on her left lapel.

One time I asked her straight out: 'Roie, why are you pretending to be a witch?'

'Christ, Eileen,' she replied, with great dignity, 'I *am* a witch.'

Witch or no, she was a true original, and a great friend to me those first days out of home.

Much to my delight, I found a sort of family within the walls of the Phillip Street cottage and its courtyard. A feeling of belonging – which I'd lost when my father started drinking – began to rekindle with my friends. We would run to each other on the slightest whim to borrow some rouge, or some milk, or to share something fascinating we had just discovered.

We introduced each other to interesting people we met along the way. Class distinction was important in Australia at that time. People tended only to socialise with their own class, but in the bohemian environment of Phillip Street I began to meet people from very different walks of life.

For example, I was introduced to the idea of a 'remittance man': a British man of means whose relatives had been embarrassed by scandal and packed him away to Australia with enough money to live a louche life, but not enough for a return passage.

A young man named Darley was a prime example. The first time I ever met him he was lounging gracefully in my neighbour Joan's only chair, sipping a glass of wine. He was an aspiring actor and had once lived on a small boat in Sydney Harbour with the actor Chips Rafferty. That is, until one or the other set the boat on fire and they had to dive overboard and swim to the Double Bay Yacht Club for safety. Over time, we all took an interest in Darley, who was the sort of man to sow chaos among impressionable women.

We were all young and quite jolly, exploring what it meant to be an adult in the world, away from the confines of family.

This was the first time I'd lived away from my mother. It was a time of learning, of creating my own family, and of growing into my own self. I had the freedom to talk about art and culture, my interests, feelings, desires.

For a young woman interested in the arts, it was a rich life, even if we weren't rich ourselves. Our courtyard was full of fascinating company, and close to all the places I needed and wished to visit. I loved scrappy Phillip Street, pristine Macquarie. Back in 1936 there were fewer cars about, so the streets were quieter, except for the trams that rattled by every half an hour. The world was at our feet. The Art Gallery, the Botanic Gardens, the public library, the cafes and teahouses of the city – all a short walk away.

In Adyar House on Bligh Street a cinema showed European – mainly French – films, and Roie and our friends would occasionally go to see one as a group. If any French was spoken in the movie, our resident remittance man Darley would interpret loudly for us, mainly to show off, until someone in the back row would shout: 'Shut up down there! Or we'll come over and shut you up!'

There was a vegetarian restaurant downstairs from the cinema, run by two elderly theosophist ladies, one of whom was shaky. Her head and her hands shook so much we expected to see lettuce leaves float through the air on the way to the salad bowls. One of my friends offered to help but she turned him down with, 'No, thank you, dear. We get help from the other side.'

Supernatural or not, they served some of the nicest salads in Sydney, so we didn't mind too much how dinner came together.

Everything I could wish for was on my doorstep. From my room, I would stroll to the corner of our street, cross over to Bent Street, walk past the library and I would be almost at the Conservatorium where I studied. I enjoyed this ritual – walking under the palm trees and entering into the world of music – although by now I had doubts about my future as an opera singer.

On my regular walk one day, I recall passing two people I took to be very old (probably in their sixties!) sitting on a park bench. The man was trying to persuade the woman to let him kiss her. She was acting coy, but I felt quite sure they would soon kiss. This was a revelation to me, because I'd thought that sexual desire ended at the age of thirty-five. I continued on my way in a state of wonder at just how long one would be at the mercy of desire in this life.

One morning on the way to class, I noticed an intriguing little archway entrance to the building at 173 Macquarie Street. On the wall, a brass plate advertised the services of 'Dr Richard Want, Psychoanalyst'.

I'd heard this Dr Want on the radio, speaking on the subject of Sigmund Freud and the unconscious mind. I was intrigued. What dark secrets might lurk in my unconscious mind? I made inquiries, and within two weeks had an appointment to undergo analysis.

When I arrived for my first appointment, I was expecting an old man. A professorial type with heavy spectacles and a bushy beard. When Dr Want answered the door, he was very different – a young man of about thirty, with clear skin and serious grey eyes.

I remember telling Dr Want my dreams. One in which a wild white horse with black markings ran away with me and another rather darker one about snakes slithering about in a muddy pool. As a Freudian, he must have thought he'd hit the jackpot.

I went back to the courtyard that night and told Roie, as well as our friends Anne and Joan, about my adventure into psychoanalysis. We sat up and drank Pimm's No. 1 to celebrate my journey to the brink of sanity.

Shortly after the third month, Dr Richard Want told me he would have to stop the analysis because he wanted to ask me to go out with him. I had a feeling this would eventually happen, so the development did not come as a surprise. I was thrilled to death; I'd known a few young men in my teenage years in Coogee, but I had never had a lover.

We went to the Metropolitan Hotel for drinks and dinner. I wore one of my most stylish dresses and felt terribly sophisticated, sitting in a deep, cosy couch, sipping a cocktail with an attractive older man in a smart hotel. I was only slightly startled to learn Richard was married.

Richard had a wife (from whom he was now separated) and a son (who lived with his mother). Once upon a time the three of them had lived in a big house in Woollahra, but now Richard was living in his rooms on Macquarie Street. Richard and his wife were civilised individuals and quite liked each other, but they no longer wished to be married. They considered themselves above petty notions like jealousy and bitterness. He had a PhD in Freudian psychology, and she had an interest in the teachings of Indian philosopher Krishnamurti. They each thought they'd found a path to psychological freedom. For my part, I thought this was all very modern and liberated.

One day Richard took me to his former family home to meet his estranged wife. Jean was an attractive woman and a smart dresser. On this occasion, she wore a blue silk dress with a white pique collar. It went with a very ingenious kind of headscarf that turned into a hat when tied around one's head. This was the last word in fashion, and it impressed me more than anything else I had heard about her. She was a bit older than me, and I felt a little like I was being introduced to a schoolteacher.

It suddenly struck me that this was an odd thing; to be taken home to meet your lover's wife. It had not occurred to me before that they might still have feelings about the breakup of their marriage. Richard and Jean retired to a back room to talk privately. The conversation went on for quite a long time and I heard her whisper to him, 'Have you seduced her yet?'

He hadn't, as it happened. But somehow there was an understanding between us that we should probably have a sexual relationship. We knew that if we were to be 'going out' together then that would include sleeping together. There was no long courtship. We had discussed the matter of sex and decided that we would 'do it'. But so far, it had been purely theoretical.

I was uneducated in matters of the heart – and in the physical act of lovemaking. I recall a conversation with Roie about two of our temporary neighbours in the Phillip Street apartments – a man and a woman who moved in with their piano and ambitions to write a musical 'about centaurs'.

The man had a wonky back, and required an elaborate device attached to the bed in order to sleep. I wondered aloud how they managed to go about their business without being able to lie flat on the bed.

'Christ, Eileen,' said Roie, quite exasperated. 'Can't you say sex?'

'Well, all right, Roie, well, sex. What do you think they do?'

Roie couldn't say. We had no answers, which goes to show that we didn't know about all the odd ways that men and women (and men and men, and women and women, and on it goes) manage in the never-ending pursuit of happiness. All we had even surmised was the most basic and classic method.

In the 1930s, we didn't have sexual freedom, so you could stay young for a long time. And frustrated. And guilty. The fear of sex had been instilled in me by my mother, who had been led to believe that 'men would do anything to get what they wanted'.

She need not have worried. Richard wanted what was best for me. He was less a predatory animal than a kindly housecat and knew nothing about the art of seduction. Honest to a fault, he was not interested in devious ways. He was forthright, with an almost intellectual approach to sex. I believe that his own sexual education came from Freud. After completing his PhD and becoming a celebrated professional, Richard was able to understand woman theoretically, but not so much emotionally or physically. His nickname for me, 'Krambo', was perhaps evidence of this. It is the sort of name one gives to a schoolmate, or a sandwich. Not one that should necessarily be invoked in a fit of passion.

I really loved Richard, but even after we consummated our relationship, we never quite experienced the passion that I yearned for. After a while, we were able to acquit ourselves in that regard, but afterwards he would always ask, 'Was that all right, Krambo?'

Physical matters aside, though, I was quite happy with Richard, and he was a wonderful friend and confidante.

It was 47.8 degrees, the hottest day for the past fifty years in Sydney, when Richard and I had lunch at The Spotted Dog restaurant on Macquarie Street. We drank cool drinks and ate delicious cold salads and talked about what we were going to do with our future.

His divorce had come through and he was now a free man. I didn't feel particularly pressed to get married. I already had Richard and could be with him every day if I wished. Besides, since we lived so close by to one another it was almost as if we *were* married.

By the time we reached dessert, I glanced down at the windowsill and noticed a bee staggering about as though it was on its last legs. It couldn't even crawl in a straight line, and it certainly couldn't fly. It looked to me as though it was dehydrated.

Without conscious intention, I took my brooch and punched a hole into a grape on my plate, so that a bubble of juice burst out of the top. I placed the grape like a waiter in front of the bee and was quite excited when I saw its tongue shoot out, straight into the bubble of juice, which then very quickly disappeared as the bee drank its fill.

Richard was busy eating and not watching what was happening, but I was transfixed. After stumbling about for a few more seconds, the bee extended its wings, steadied itself and flew straight up and out the window, in the direction of the Botanic Gardens across the road.

A sense of great satisfaction came over me and I turned to Richard, who by this time was looking inquiringly at me. 'Look, Richard,' I said, 'Look at that bee flying away to the Botanic Gardens! Aren't you pleased that I saved its life?'

He looked at me, smiled, and said, 'Clever girl, Krambo.'

These were the greatest moments with Richard. The little ones. We would spend four years happily together, and it was a tender and loving time. He was my friend. On learning a bit more about Freud, I should say that he was also somewhat of a father figure to me.

On reflection, it was inevitable that we would part one day. Young as I was, I sometimes made choices that showed how naive I was in the ways of the world.

One time I went to a movie with a young man and, despite having no romantic interest, invited him back for tea. It was all quite friendly, until Richard burst in.

'Oh, hello, Richard,' was all I could think to say. 'Would you like a cup of tea?'

The three of us sat there trying to think of some topic of conversation until the other man left. Richard followed shortly after, his jealousy unresolved.

Darley, the 'remittance man' who had become a regular feature at Phillip Street and had popped up over the years, began to take an interest in me.

He and I began a slow romance. Richard didn't like him and understood him to be bad news. As did I. But the fact that a person is forbidden fruit does not make them less appealing. At times we are drawn towards the thing we should not choose. He had taken the room next to mine, so it was only a matter of time.

Poor Richard must have known. One night I heard him ask the landlady if I was home, and soon afterward knocked on the door for a long time. On the other side of the door, Darley and I froze until Richard left.

Richard and I had dinner that night, and he didn't say anything. Now, with the benefit of hindsight, I can understand that Richard was a shy young man who was uncertain with women.

Eventually, Richard began to have his own dalliance, and we bit the bullet.

'I think we must part, Krambo,' he said, and, as we always did, we discussed it intellectually. I really did love him, but he told me that if we ever actually married, then I would always be looking for more, physically. The reality was that the passion I'd read about in French novels just didn't exist between us.

I wasn't prepared to fight for our relationship because I knew it had to end. I went back to my own room. The sense of loss was strong. For months I grieved and would wake up with the startling feeling that something awful had happened. But as the days wore on, the feeling would fade. As months passed, the hurt grew less.

Meanwhile, Darley, the aspiring actor, promptly exited stage left. Some weeks after I became 'single', Darley moved out of the room next door and, in true Darley fashion, vanished forever.

It was the end of my life with Richard. Although of course something of Richard was to stay with me forever. That is the way with first love. That is the way with all love.

I realise now that Richard gave me something I sorely needed at that age. I was in my twenties and discovering the world through our relationship. I had not had much education at school and in many ways, he was my teacher. With his guidance, I was able to mature enough so that, when the real, great, true passion that would shape my life came along, I would be ready.

Three years later, after I had become a professional dancer, I was given a dance called 'Farewell'. It was a poetic, beautiful work about two souls parting, saying goodbye forever, set to heart-wrenching music by the Russian Romantic-era composer Modest Mussorgsky. I was enriched by bittersweet sorrow when I performed it.

I danced it with different partners over the years, but in my mind I always thought of Richard. In some ways, he was my first dance partner, and the time we spent together is a gift I carry with me always. I thought of 'Farewell' as his dance. Our dance. The sorrow of our parting, born anew into something beautiful. And it was beautiful.

Chapter Three

Meeting Madame / The Ecstasy of Purpose

I N THE LATE 1930S, FOR THOSE OF US IN OUR EARLY twenties, nobody seemed to own anything, or live in the same place for too long. One December, in the midst of a scorching summer, an infestation of bedbugs overcame our Phillip Street Courtyard, and my friends and I fled to other apartments.

When the summer was over, we happily reconvened back to the courtyard and life went on. But in my absence, another person had moved into the room upstairs and I had to take a smaller one downstairs. This room featured heavy walls of bare stone with no real windows, and it opened directly onto the courtyard without even a doorstep. It wasn't designed for a young woman to live in. Not even an animal. It was hard to imagine what its original purpose had been, unless it was a storeroom for horses' saddles.

When my mother first saw this room, she looked at it with disbelief and, I suspect, some dismay. I'm not sure if she wholly approved of what she saw at Phillip Street, but she put on a brave face. She would exchange pleasantries with whoever was about and was polite about the demonic painting that peeked through Roie's open doorway.

'Eileen lives in a historical house on Phillip Street with some strange people,' she would tell her friends. 'They're all very nice. They seem to seem to like her, but . . . I don't know . . . at least it's close to the Conservatorium.'

My mother would visit now and again during her weekly trip to town to go shopping or have tea with friends. She favoured the fashionable restaurants on Pitt Street. Sometimes I would join her, wearing a silk dress I had made myself especially for such occasions. I would meet her in the foyer of Cahill's, where they served ice-cream cake topped with thick whipped cream and a caramel sauce that was a revelation to Sydney diners at the time.

On special occasions, she took me to the theatre, and it was one of these nights that would change the course of my life dramatically.

It started, as all life-defining events should, with a good meal. Mother and I met for dinner at Florentine, an Italian restaurant on Castlereagh Street. Mario, the proprietor, rightly took great pride in his food, particularly his ravioli, minestrone and zabaglione. He was a real Italian restaurateur, rare in Sydney back then.

From there, we took a taxi to the Conservatorium for a charity concert.

The program was for a mixed concert of singing, violin music and dancing, and it singled out one act for special notice: six dancers from the Bodenwieser Ballet.

I'd heard of the company and had even met Madame Bodenwieser briefly on a social visit to a friend's apartment. On first meeting, I had no idea that this small, dark woman who gazed at me through a gold-rimmed lorgnette – those handheld spectacles in vogue at the time – was fated to shape my entire life. Nor did I truly understand the tragic fate that had brought her to Sydney – the despair and destruction in Europe that had set her on a path to bring so much joy and fulfilment to me and others like me in Australia.

In the beginning, the war did not affect our lives in Phillip Street too much. We became aware of food rationing, but we ate like field mice already. Silk stockings became scarce, but then available on the black market. Not long after that, men from around Sydney began donning their slouch hats and heading off, some never to return. Then came the refugees from Europe, mostly Jewish.

Among these refugees was Gertrud Bodenwieser. When she arrived in Sydney, joined by some of her dancers, she brought with her the very avant-garde modernist dance that Europe had to offer. This was her gift to Sydney, and the tool with which she carved out a new life for herself. Audiences in Australia were completely unfamiliar with her style, but it was greeted with appreciation and amazement.

Since arriving in Australia, Madame Bodenwieser had put on frequent recitals and contributed to fundraising concerts for the war effort, and it was one of these charity concerts my mother had taken me to.

During the interval, I went for a wander. As a Conservatorium student, I was familiar with the auditorium and I was curious. I passed through a door and walked down a corridor that led to the side of the stage. I'd been in this corridor many times. I wasn't looking for anyone in particular – to be honest I didn't know many of my fellow students all that well. Singing and piano classes were rather solitary. So I didn't encounter anyone I knew, but the young women I did see would end up becoming as close to me as sisters in the coming years.

The Bodenwieser dancers were making their way along the corridor with an air of confidence and purpose. Their gaze was fixed on the stage door, and they seemed beautiful, remote, as though they were in a world entirely of their own making. They didn't cast a single glance at anyone else. Certainly they didn't notice me, standing mute in admiration.

One dancer was particularly striking: a dark, bewitching wraith. I was quite in awe of her. Her eyelids were dark and shiny in the soft light, her mouth a slash of crimson. This was, I would learn, the preference of Madame Bodenwieser – for her dancers to style themselves in the manner of silent film-stars, in a way that would show dramatically both on stage and in photographs – 'Zee mouth should be a scarlet wound!' she would cry.

This all came later. At the time I didn't even realise the dancer was heavily made up. Her face was not like that of women I knew from Sydney; it was the face of a glamorous, tigerish character from a novel. Her name was Evelyn Ippen. Close behind her followed another, much smaller, more modest and soft-featured young woman with long dark hair. This was Bettina Vernon. They would become my friends and colleagues, but in that moment they seemed to come from another world.

After the six women trailed a harried-looking man carrying armfuls of costumes. Behind him came another man, cradling sheets of musical score as though they were the most precious items on Earth. He raced along in his dapper suit, muttering, 'I'm late, I'm late,' like the White Rabbit. This was Marcel Lorber, the famous composer and long-time colleague of Madame. The procession through the stage door, and the chimes signalling the end of interval called me back to my seat next to my mother.

The curtain rose, revealing two girls bathed in soft blue light. They were curled up together as tightly as a furled rosebud. With the hems of their sheer organza costumes spread around them, they did in fact look like a single flower. Then, as the first bars of the famous 'Blue Danube' waltz rang out, the flower started to bloom. A shiver of movement like a breeze across a bough. Four arms, light as the air, slowly extended, and two lovely faces turned upwards, tendrils of hair loose across their cheeks, like flowers towards the sun.

At that point, Evelyn waltzed onto the stage. With her back to the audience, her face turned from me, I could see where her hair, cut shorter than the other dancers, met the elegant nape of her neck. Her neck was striking, and very beautiful. This was not lost on her, I would discover later. 'Men like the nape of the neck,' she would tell me. But in that moment, I felt her charm intensely. On stage Evelyn had transformed from tiger-woman to a form as graceful and flowing as the Danube herself. Two more dancers joined her, then another, until six girls in billowing blue costumes swirled across the stage, forming patterns in a kind of dance I had never seen before.

It seemed to me, sitting rapt in the audience, that the dance itself was alive. As though the breath that animated the bodies of the dancers had taken on a life of its own. I could almost feel its force in my own body as I watched. I left the concert with my head spinning, hardly able to say a word to my mother. Whatever it is in the soul that recognises its own told me that this dance was for me. That night, I resolved that I would do whatever was needed to join this new world.

Until that moment it had never occurred to me that I wanted to be a dancer. All of a sudden, it seemed my sole purpose in life. I'd had a few classes as a child, and they didn't satisfy me very much. But as soon as I saw Madame's work, I knew that this was what I'd been waiting for.

'The Blue Danube' was beautiful and flowing and expressive and not at all tight and rigid, I just fell in love with it. Another dance they performed at the concert was 'The Slavonic', wearing great big skirts with large motifs on them. The dancers took wonderful poses that looked as though they were accidental, but of course it was carefully composed art. Even in my naivety, I could sense that.

The emotions I experienced that night – seeing Madame Bodenwieser's heart expressed through her dancers – were hard to describe; it was like the feeling between two people who've met before, in another lifetime. This was the world for me.

In the morning, I went in search of Madame Bodenwieser and found her on King Street, where she had set up a temporary studio for her dance company. I arrived just as a rehearsal was beginning. Madame, up close, was a tiny woman. She seemed tinier still against her statuesque dancers, with her hair pulled back in a severe style. She wore black satin pants with a white blouse and took no notice of me. Her attention was with the piano, where she sat.

She was deep in conversation with Marcel, the composer. It seemed like an argument; they were speaking in German, so it would go and on and on and she would say, 'No, Marci, no, Marci,' and he'd say, 'But, Madame, but, Madame.'

The dancers from 'The Blue Danube' performance at the charity concert were milling about, chattering away in German. One of them, small, strong and stunning – reminiscent of nothing so much as a golden goddess – approached me. I told her I wanted to become a student of their company. So, I was introduced to Madame, and boldly told her: 'Madame, I would like to learn dancing from you.'

Madame lifted her lorgnette and examined me for a long moment. Finally she said she would have to see me in action. Marcel would play something for me, and I would show her what I could do, if I had any 'talent for the dance'.

On her instruction, Marcel began to tease some music from the piano. I'm not sure where I found the courage, but somehow, I felt I knew what I had to do. Moving to the music, I expressed myself as best I could. Practically, that meant that I sort of floated around, waving my arms, lifting a leg and putting it down again, doing a little hop.

Madame watched on, and afterwards gave me a kind look. 'That was *schön*.' She told me she saw something of a dancer in me, and that she saw potential in me as a dance teacher. Then she asked if I wanted to study to become one.

'I want to study, but not to be a teacher,' I replied, 'to be a dancer. I want to be a dancer in your group.'

I remember the smile she gave me, which seemed to say, *Oh yes, and so would many others.*

This was not the response I'd hoped for, but it was encouragement enough. I went home in great excitement, got out an old black dress, cut it to thigh-length and replaced the seams with loose georgette.

This was to be my regulation costume, and I wore it to my first class the very next day.

※

I don't remember much about the very first class; what I remember are the personalities in the dressing-room afterwards. When I first became a student of Madame Gertrud Bodenwieser, her small group of most trusted dancers were Austrian girls who had been members of her company in Vienna.

Evelyn Ippen was part of this inner circle, and she was just as formidable offstage as on. She was a beautiful, emotional dancer with a strong and exotic presence – still in the Bodenwieser style, yet full of her own irrepressible nature. Bettina Vernon was also part of this group. She was petite, but a powerful dancer, and kind and practical as could be. Then there was Emmy Towsey (Taussig), who was capable of the most pure, gentle expression on stage. She was a great actress – she could control her attractive face, and dance divinely – but was tough, political and indomitable backstage.

'Anyone got a cigarette for me?' she would announce, walking into a group, and I would be scandalised. Fancy a woman asking for a cigarette? It was Emmy I tried to emulate most as a dancer, although she was a bit bigger than me. She had a rebellious streak I much admired.

These girls, mostly Jewish, had escaped when the Nazis invaded Austria. They were phenomenal. They had lived through so much, and barely escaped death, and now danced in a way that expressed the full force of their experiences. Then there was Shona Dunlop, who was from New Zealand, but had travelled to Vienna to study with Madame. There were others too – Australian girls, who, like me, had fallen under Madame's spell.

All the girls were so devoted to Madame, and such wonderful dancers. In that first class, I was so dazzled by them that I hardly noticed the time passing. All I remember was the feeling of freedom, the sense of joy in movement I felt as I started to learn my first Bodenwieser technique. That and the feeling of ecstasy when I left the class. At the end of two hours, I floated out of the studio and down Pitt Street. I felt that I was barely in my body at all, or rather that my body was comprised of pure joy.

Until Madame came into my life, I had not known how to truly release myself through art. Singing, piano, theory – I could manage well enough behind the scenes, but on stage, performing an aria for example, I grew tighter and tighter. Bodenwieser dance released me.

Madame Bodenwieser's way of teaching was truly unique. She would share her knowledge with you in such a gentle way you didn't know the importance of what you were learning until you had already mastered it.

Her lessons were magical because you hardly knew they were happening. She would introduce you to a movement as a form of exercise, and, through daily practise, the movement would become a part of you. Not that it was undisciplined – Madame's dance had an unbreakable core of discipline – but the style was expressive rather than controlled. Movement created expression, and in turn this created form and drama.

A class would begin quite practically – with physical exercises, lined up at the barre, very similar to the warmups of classical ballet. For about ten minutes we would move our foot in and out of position, practise holding our balance, shifting our weight back and forth, while Marcel played his rhythmic 'one and two and three' music.

Marcel's piano was angled in such a way that he could see the whole class over its rim and keep time for us. He was a very accomplished composer and performer, but he would plunk out a very simple little rhythm for the sake of us dancers.

I found that music quite boring at the time, but even now I will sing it to myself when I am exercising on my own. Even if it was dull, we had to keep our face and expression alive and alert. I still do that too. Expression becomes a way of living.

Once we were warmed up, we would move to the floor, and begin what Madame called 'Free Movement'. That is perhaps not the most accurate description – all of Madame's classes were planned, but even so we would study abstract, flowing movements. As I practised them, it did not feel like work, or study, but the purest play. Just wonderful movements that filled me with joy.

From the basic shapes of her dance, Madame created a way to tap into a cosmic sort of joy. She had what she called 'ecstasy of purpose' – an ability to sense the potential to bring a dance into the world, and then to manifest it.

We learned that the movement came from within and extended to the very fingertips. Breath carried the movement, the subtlest of communication. She was talking to the onlooker, yes, but also to fellow dancers. We learned a sort of secret language: how to relate to each other, to complement each other's movements.

Our teacher had a great appreciation of each student's individual talent. She fostered one's exceptionality, while at the same time creating a group of dancers who could work, in a way, as one body. We learned to lean on each other, to touch and make contact without any embarrassment.

This was perhaps Madame's greatest genius – to take the raw thread of a single dancer's potential, and to make it work in concert.

Madame gave us a physical vocabulary with which to express a range of emotions. With the Bodenwieser movements at our fingertips, we could spring into action to convey any idea that Madame directed us to. This was what made her such a prolific and intuitive choreographer – she would bring an artfully composed idea to class, but as she drew the performance from us, we would naturally make our own contributions and improvisations to better express the meaning behind the dance. Each dance was a true collaboration with a great mind. We were loyal and grateful as a result. Everyone who had the privilege of working with her was.

Marcel was one of her most loyal allies. His music in these classes – once he'd moved on from his *plunk plunk plunk* and into his real work – was inspiring. From long association with dancers, and Madame in particular, he was able to compose short pieces that expressed exactly what she wanted for certain expressive movements and combinations of movement. He could even improvise music specific to each dancer – to encourage us to express our own individuality in improvisational classes.

By the time we began to work with Madame on the construction of dance works, much of what she asked of us came easily, or even automatically.

Madame spoke about movement as an essential force of life. How it comes from the people and springs from their impulses and feelings, and is transformed into an art form by the artists. From the very first classes, and each time we began to study a new work, expression and energy were as important as the composition of the dance. We did our best to illustrate with improvisation. In doing so, we performed works of such beauty that we astonished ourselves.

At times, when I danced, I felt as if my spirit was rising to take the place of my body. Most of Madame's work gave me that feeling. It was a revelation; you have this transcendent feeling inside you and never know – until someone comes along and shows you how to express it in dance. It was the most wonderful sensation I've ever encountered.

In the late forties several Bodenwieser dances were filmed for a documentary called *Spotlight on Australian Ballet*, and it was then I truly understood Madame's worth as a teacher. Watching our company dance 'The Blue Danube' on screen awoke in me a new appreciation for our performance. Until I saw the style, composition, and excellence of our performance through the eye of the camera, I had not truly understood what I was absorbing from our teacher. We were beautiful. And if we saw ourselves as beautiful, it was Madame we had to thank, for her training was a way to write beauty of style and spirit into being.

As I progressed further along my journey from Bodenwieser student to dancer, Evelyn and Bettina took me to the Viennese coffee house downstairs to welcome me into their group. I was so touched by their kindness.

It is hard to understand now how cosmopolitan and sophisticated it felt to be in a coffee house back then. A place that served strong coffee and cream alongside little European biscuits. We always went before rehearsal, and university students and dancers would gather in there and talk and talk and talk.

We would discuss the philosophy of all we were experiencing. I found the spiritual side of what we were doing enthralling and wanted to discuss it all properly – over Viennese coffee, with Viennese artists. Once or twice I tried to engage Madame herself in this discussion, but she had no real interest or desire to carry on such conversations, even though she may have understood what was going on in my mind.

'Yes, dear,' was all she'd say. 'But it will be better if you prepare for rehearsal.'

So I would shut up and go straight to the dressing room to prepare for rehearsal. After all, that too was rewarding. It was what she had to give.

Madame's approach to work was, from long experience, uncluttered. Besides, she had read all the great Western philosophers and the poets and the modern European novelists and had heard all those discussions in the famous coffee houses in Vienna long ago. In other words, she was way ahead of us.

I still think deeply about art and culture and what it means to be human and alive. I ponder over the question of a dance. It does not exist until you do it. And when you do it, it hardly exists, for as each step is taken it passes, and is no longer there. It has passed into a new step, and then that passes too. So what is a dance?

Music can be written, so can a song. But how can a dance be written down?

I know there are systems of dance notation. But how can the breath, expression and the floating of an arm through air ever be put on paper? A Bodenwieser dance is a body's conversation with the air itself. How does one translate that to words?

When we had to learn a dance that Madame had choreographed back in Vienna, she remembered everything. A dance never ceases to be. It's always waiting in the dark ready to be brought forth again.

Dance began long before humanity itself evolved. A leaf dances on the tree. Water dances down the river. Stars dance above us, giving us light. Atoms dance, inside us, giving us life. Giving us purpose. Giving us ecstasy.

Chapter Four

Life Class / Art and Dance

UNFORTUNATELY, NO AMOUNT OF ECSTATIC purpose in life will pay the rent. My rent was modest, but 'modest' is an infinite amount when one has no money at all. The truth was, although I spent my days studying the mysteries of dance with Madame, I still had to make a living.

I had started to get work as an artist's model back when I lived in the Phillip Street courtyard, and this had turned out to be a profession I enjoyed. In fact, I would find myself relying on it to pay the rent at many points in my life and in many cities all over the world. It taught me a fair amount of what I know about art, as well.

It was Anne D'Arcy who had first introduced me to the work. Her mother came from New Orleans, and had given Anne her dark eyes, soft hair and easy, slow laugh. She was a good neighbour – cheerful, kind and boisterous. Sometimes she held court over us like a jolly queen. As a model, she was in high demand and posed for artists of renown in Sydney. She was very happy in her occupation, her life, and didn't aspire to be anything more.

Roie, who also worked as a model, looked at her work differently. She was an artist in her own right who, like me, modelled simply to pay the rent.

If you know what you're looking for, you'll see Roie and Anne pop up among the works of that fevered age of Australian modernist art. And now and again, you might see me.

~

My first engagement was for the painter Norman Lindsay; Anne had asked me to take her place because she had a bad cold. I went with no expectations. I was not very aware of his paintings at that time, but Anne and Roie had told me he was a celebrity in the art world.

The studio was on Bent Street. I rang the doorbell and summoned a shy little man who turned out to be Mr Lindsay himself. It was hard to imagine a less frightening person. Later on, when I became familiar with his theatrical oil painting, I was amazed. I never would have expected such bold expression from someone so fragile-looking.

He brought me into a very large room with a couch in the middle. Glancing around, any nerves I had disappeared. It was all very ordinary.

He asked me to disrobe and pose, reclining on the couch. On the wrist of my outstretched arm he placed a stuffed white dove. I was intrigued by the idea of the dove sitting on my wrist. It was a playful, imaginative image that appealed to me.

Mr Lindsay observed my body, my features, my hair. At this last, he frowned. I was wearing the 'shingle', the short bob that was in fashion for young women. Mr Lindsay considered, then placed a long blonde wig on my head. After painting for a while, he looked up and said wistfully: 'Oh, it's lovely to see a woman with long hair again.'

After that first session, I became a professional artist's model. I enjoyed it, finding it much more satisfying than shining a torch around as a theatre usher, which had helped pay my rent when I first left home.

Life modelling is hard work, though. Maintaining a pose is a test of endurance. There's no such thing as holding perfectly still – when you try, parts of your body get quite busy wanting you to move to relieve the pressure. But a slight twist of the upper body or tiny shift of weight between the standing leg and the relaxed leg can alter the entire pose.

I was a good model. As a dancer, I understood movement, but I also understood the power of stillness. I came to think of posing for artists as a sort of dance frozen in time.

Life models were in high demand in Sydney at that time. The city was reflecting the art scenes of London and Paris, and there were a great number of art schools. East Sydney Technical College was the biggest, and I began to get regular work there. Soon I was posing for classes all around Sydney.

In a single week I might be at Julian Ashton's Sydney Art School in The Rocks and also at Dattilo Rubbo's studio in another part of the city. It was not the best arrangement, as the models had to go back to collect their pay the next week and by then we were modelling somewhere else. I had to be precise with my booking diary as the jobs were all in different locations and at different times.

It was easy to lose track of the schedule. I once arrived at an art class and began to disrobe before I realised that another model was already in position. There was a long silence until I put my dress on again and left.

I was so busy, and so absorbed in my first year of Bodenwieser dance classes, that I gave almost no thought to romance. Until one day, it happened.

I met my cubist.

⁂

Rah Fizelle was a well-known painter in Sydney art circles and some of his works were on permanent exhibition in the Art Gallery of New South Wales. He had a studio and an apartment in one of the houses on lower George Street.

I met him through Anne D'Arcy – another occasion when she had asked me to take her place for a booking. Over the next two weeks, as I sat for him and he worked, our sessions were silent. In that silence, though, the feeling between us began to grow, and it blossomed into a sweet and real love.

Rah was different from Richard. He was older than me by sixteen years, but he was passionate. There was not so much talking, which felt refreshing to me. This time I really felt I was in love, the way a man and a woman love each other, with an element that had been missing in my love for Richard.

There was a quality in it of seriousness and a belief in the depth of feeling we experienced. Although some people might've said it was just an ordinary love affair, to me it was about the closest thing to heaven. There was also something that made me think of the romances of the Bohemians of Paris – a certain sense of doom or sadness, or of impossibility.

Rah and I were at very different stages of life. I had only just found my calling as a dancer, while Rah was an established artist.

At that time, cubism was the new thing. Even the David Jones window dresser had made a display of it in the corner window, facing Hyde Park. It featured two larger than life figures composed of cubes and triangles, dressed in similarly patterned silk dresses, and it caused a sensation. People walking by stopped to gasp in wonder. When I saw it, I understood a little of what it was meaning to say, from having seen Rah at work.

We didn't go out very often but one afternoon we went for a walk through a reserve on the opposite side of the harbour, where there were flowering shrubs and graceful trees with fine slim trunks and clusters of soft green leaves, and lots of birds. As we passed one of the shrubs, I picked a flower and carried it a short distance along the path. Then I wished I hadn't picked it because it was a delicate flower, and I could see it would soon wilt in my hand. I didn't want that to happen, so, as we passed another shrub, I placed it on a branch, back with its fellow flowers. I didn't think Rah was taking any notice of what I was doing, but then I heard him say, 'That was a nice thing to do, Eileen.' It was not a remarkable thing for me to do, or for him to say, but I treasured his remark and was glad I'd pleased him.

It was such a pure and easy love. So what went wrong? Nothing, really, except, I suppose, that Rah had another woman in his life.

One evening I was at Rah's place having dinner. He had specially cooked a baked dinner for me – rich and moist with salty, fatty gravy, baked potatoes, pumpkin, green peas and onions that had been cooked almost to the point of melting around the meat – which we began to eat, sitting together on the edge of his bed.

Then – and if this were a film instead of a story, the music would swell and a clashing of chords would signal that something heartbreaking was about to happen – out of nowhere, a woman, quite a bit older than I, walked in uninvited. She didn't say anything – no 'hello' or 'it's me' or anything like that – but crossed the room, picked up something from a small table, turned and walked back out.

We went on with our dinner as if nothing had happened. But I had felt her glance as she left us there, together. It was strange I didn't feel curious, nor did I ask for any explanation and he didn't offer any, and yet deep down I must have understood what had happened and why. This was a woman who had been in a relationship with my new lover long before I came into his life. By walking into the private part of his studio, I imagine she was letting him know that she knew about us. And letting me know that Rah and I were only temporary.

Several days later, I went alone to a concert at the Conservatorium to hear someone we all knew play the piano. As I sat for a while in the lobby before going back to the hall after interval, I saw Rah with a group of people including the woman from that night. I understood then that it was over.

We didn't have a big drama-filled breakup. The next time we met as usual, Rah talked to me about what had happened. He appeared to be more disturbed than I was; he said it mattered because my feelings must have been hurt. I said no. She did have right on her side, and our beautiful relationship could never be permanent.

A bit later I came home one evening and found him lying on my bed. 'I was so tired,' he said. 'You've never seen me so tired, Eileen.' I let him rest there for a while, and he fell asleep. I thought his tiredness might have been to do with the conflict he must have been going through. When he woke up, he said he was sorry, so we had our second parting.

In our short time together, I had learned a great deal and was not very much hurt when I knew I had to let him go. I felt a little sad, but I didn't believe it could have been otherwise.

And truly, at the time, my heart belonged to Madame. I worked hard, and soon I was assigned my first solo dance to be performed at our student concert. Madame choreographed the solo for me. It was called 'Spring'. When she began to create the dance, I was overcome with emotion. I was almost shaking.

She showed me some of the poses she wanted for the beginning of the dance but encouraged me to make my own contributions. The act of creating a dance was a great mystery to me. I was sure I would not know how, but such was the genius of Madame's technique: my body already held the knowledge of the dance I was to learn – everything I needed, literally, at my fingertips.

Madame choreographed easily, and the dance was fully composed at that first session. It was physically undemanding – a student's dance, with nothing disturbing or physically arduous. To look upon, it was charming and easy; a lovely, dreamy expression of spring. Its simplicity only made me love it more. To complement the choreography, I created my own costume, inspired by Botticelli's painting *La Primavera*. A simple costume for an innocent dance. It was wonderful for Madame to have created something that suited me so well; it felt as if she had quenched in me a long, deep thirst.

I fully expected everyone who saw me perform 'Spring' to feel the same way. I was excited for the praise I thought would come my way after the performance. My mother was impressed – pleased to see me floating about in the manner of a Botticelli spring maiden. More than anything, I think she was pleased I'd found something that made my life so full. I felt as if my joy could be read by the audience.

However, after the performance, while basking in praise, a family acquaintance came up to me with a sort of shudder of distaste. Her name was Mrs Collins. 'I didn't like your dance,' she said, quite bluntly.

I must have looked quite shocked as I blurted out, 'Why not?'

'It was,' she said, with her look of disgust deepening, '*too sexy.*'

Too sexy! Can you imagine? I was distraught.

That night I lay sleepless until late, dwelling on what Mrs Collins had said, and the expression on her face. I couldn't believe her comment about my beloved dance. Too sexy? The feeling I'd had on stage had been sensuous, but sexy? I felt it was pure, not voluptuous. I did not believe my dance had been too tantalising, or overly sentimental – both possibilities that I could imagine would repel some people.

In spite of all the positive praise I'd received, I thought only of this one negative critique by Mrs Collins. In the end, I decided the fault must lie with me. 'I desire approval so much,' I told myself over and over, 'that I just can't accept it when someone reacts in that way.' The dance had come to mean so much to me, and I felt that for someone to dislike it must mean that they didn't like me. It took me some time to realise I'd fallen into this trap, which is something any kind of artist would be best avoiding.

Really, Mrs Collins' appraisal of my dance had less to do with me than with her. To watch a young dancer express herself with pure creative spirit and sensuality, but see only sexuality? That is a symptom of a serious lack of imagination. To create is to take the pure stuff of life, and to turn it, like straw to gold, into something beyond value – even if only the artist really appreciates the lustre.

One can never make anything great out of their life's work if they spend their time worrying about what the Mrs Collinses of the world will say.

*

Madame rarely took any notice of what anyone said. She was far too absorbed in her creative work. I learned from her in that respect. You go ahead and do your work, and if it has any value, someone will notice it. It certainly will not be valuable if you work to try to please your critics, because half of your creative energy will be used up worrying about them. Every time I have taken a wrong turn trying to please someone, I end up regretting it. One can only follow the shape of the work as it presents itself. When it is all done, and you have brought the work into the world, you realise – we need not have worried.

Chapter Five

Australian Tours / In Good Company

After three years of training, Madame finally elevated me from a student to a member of the company. I had been refashioned from an ordinary young girl into a Bodenwieser dancer. By then, Madame Bodenwieser had established herself and her studio on Pitt Street. In doing so, she brought to Sydney not only the height of modernist dance, but sophistication of a sort my fellow dancers from Australia had never known. We became aware that such a way of life existed through our everyday relationship with Madame and her European dancers.

In Vienna, Madame had been 'Frau Professor' – respected teacher of dance and a creative artist of renown. Although her circumstances as a refugee in Australia were somewhat more modest, she held the deportment of what used to be known as a 'grande dame'. Her manners were impeccable, her countenance carefully composed and dignified, and she was well-spoken in her sometimes quaint English, even in the face of the comparatively crude decorum of her Australian students.

When conducting a class on strong movements, which involved stomping the floor with the balls of our feet, she would urge us to 'Stamp on zee balls!' This caused us no end of mirth, matched only by the dismay of the waiters in the Viennese coffee house downstairs, whose chandeliers shook and creaked each time we stomped.

If Madame was exasperated by our childishness, she gave no sign. In class, I very rarely heard her say anything negative to a student. She was not a critical person. Her praise, when she gave it, though, was a joy. When one had excelled, finishing a dance with a trace of the sublime lingering in tired muscles, there was no higher praise than for Madame to lower her lorgnette and say, 'Very beautiful.' If she were particularly moved, she would often slip into German, so that we grew to covet the phrase '*schön*' as we would a treasure.

Madame moved naturally from English to German when touched by art. Before the war, her Vienna was rich in music, dance, painting, architecture, science, creative thought. Theatrical art flourished there, and energetic people met daily in coffee houses to discuss all manner of new creations. People gathered in the drawing rooms of cultured hostesses for feasts of music or intellectual discussion.

Although Madame had no desire to return to European society, she was determined to bring its benefits to the furthest corners of Australia. From the Pitt Street school we would set out on long tours, and it was our haven when we returned, tired but triumphant. It is no small thing to tour a dance company – even today – and Australia seemed much larger and wilder in the 1940s.

On tour, we travelled to all the major towns and cities from Brisbane to Adelaide, along dry dusty roads, coastal roads, mountainous roads and flooded roads. We visited towns in New South Wales and the chilly reaches of Victoria, and sauntered the fashionable streets of Melbourne. We went to Canberra, the Australian capital city that was barely older than we were. Up and down the glittering east coast we roamed. With the exception of Adelaide and Queensland, where the distance and weather made train travel necessary, we always travelled by bus.

We travelled across miles of Australian country, which city girls like us would probably never have seen. It took us all very far out of our comfort zones. We were hot in our summer dresses, cold in our sweaters and winter clothes.

Tours might last a fortnight, six weeks, or up to two months, depending on how many performances we gave in each town or how many towns and cities we went to. While on the road, we had to be practical, which didn't come naturally to all of us.

When we were about to leave for a tour, costumes were carefully packed in the big costume basket. Hats, if any, had their own round hat box, and shoes were packed into a canvas bag. Everything was listed and organised to make unpacking and re-packing easy each night. We were responsible for everything ourselves.

We had to pack carefully as we could not always rely on someone being available to iron costumes, especially in the smallest country towns. Evelyn Ippen, our beautiful drama queen, went so far as to suggest that some of our costumes should be taken on clothes hangers. I remember one such occasion, we had gathered at the appointed pickup spot near the entrance to the Domain at the beginning of a tour. Surrounded by our bags and with our special costumes dutifully on hangers, my mother happened to drive by at that moment in a car full of people and saw us sitting excitedly on the steps of the art gallery, while our costumes hung above us on the branches of a big tree, waving about in the breeze. The scene was rather odd, she told me later, and she had some explaining to do to her friends.

It was important to Madame that we present impeccably. We would reach a town after hours and hours of a bus navigating bumpy outback roads, and Madame would expect us in our finest wear – gloves and hats, all very proper.

As we neared our destination, we would receive the instruction from our tour manager: 'Spruce-o!' This was our signal to tidy up and make ourselves neat and attractive.

In a town full of sheep-shearers or coal miners, we would alight in our finest afternoon clothes, waving like young Princess Elizabeths. We enjoyed dressing properly; Madame expected that of us.

On my very first tour, I was in only two dances. That gave me time to pick up costumes that had been thrown on the floor in the haste that was unavoidable when a dancer had to get back on stage immediately. Apparently, no one had ever done that before. Previously, costumes had been left wherever they landed until the end of the evening's performance. I love costumes and fabrics, so I picked them up.

To my surprise I was given a bonus at the end of the tour when we were paid. Evelyn and Bettina, as senior dancers, had most of the quick changes, and they had been pleased with me. They told Madame I had been most helpful. I adored them for that, although I'm sure Madame had already noticed. Very little escaped her eye.

Madame was always with us. She was just as much a part of the performance as we were. On stage, dancing, we were aware of her standing in the wings, lorgnette up to watch every movement we made.

Her presence was an island of calm and kindness in the midst of the chaos of a dance tour.

We would all scream and yell in English, and she would come in and say, 'Quiet. Quiet, please. Zee mother speaks.' She *was* the mother and we loved her, and the particular European grace she brought into our lives.

We trailed after her into hotel lobbies like a batch of ducklings, and in turn, we looked out for her if she lost her way.

There were things about Madame that never ceased to puzzle us. On one hand she was a woman of the world, or she behaved like one. She had great respect for social conventions. On the other hand, she could be like a lost child who had her own inexplicable ways of relating to the world.

Madame could effortlessly choreograph a world-class modern dance drama without breaking a sweat, but the practicalities of life eluded her. When she wanted a taxi, she'd hail anything that moved on wheels. We were terrified to let her near a railway, because the potential for dire peril was too great. We wondered how she had come through intact from her various travails.

It took me years to understand just how capable and resilient she truly was. Madame had been in Vienna when the war broke out. She and her husband, a well-known theatrical producer, had managed to escape on the last train out of the city to Paris. Her husband was able to find work there on French radio, while Madame embarked on a prearranged tour to South America with her dance company, planning to return when the three-month tour was over. But this was not to be. With France now occupied, she could not go back to Paris, and remained in South America with her dancers for a whole year. She had no news of her husband, and lived for a long time in a terrible void. It was within that void that she came to Australia and started anew. Eventually she received news that her husband had been killed in one of the concentration camps. So she had that heartbreak to bear, and she bore it with dignity.

Although she gave no sign of her despair, I became aware of it. One evening I saw something that I never spoke of to anyone because I felt it was too private for me to spread about. Passing Madame's dressing room on my way to take my place at the barre, I happened to glance at her door. It was ajar, and there I saw Madame in bitter tears. She was sobbing quite violently. A few moments later, she was at the head of the class with Emmy beside her. She was smiling as if she had never known a moment's sorrow. Madame understood sadness and parting very well. She had great courage. I didn't think much about that at the time, but I do now.

My life had been somewhat sheltered from the horrors that were happening elsewhere in the world. The faces of the refugees from Europe held fatalistic expressions. Survival at any cost.

What can we do? We carry on. We search for a place where we can live in peace. We hold on to the art and beauty we have known, and for Madame, that was dance. For what is dance, but the opposite of horror and violence?

If the world were coarse and brutish and unsophisticated, then too bad. Madame would continue to rise to the occasion and would take the experience of Bodenwieser dance to anyone who she felt needed to experience it.

If we alighted in a town and it seemed unlikely that an audience of modern-dance aficionados would appear from the dust, Madame took it in her stride. In Canberra, for example, we arrived to find some dusty gum trees, accommodation in a hostel, and our venue – a hall next to a tiny church – on a stretch of road with no other buildings in sight. Perhaps we had been expecting some kind of science fiction metropolis from our nation's new capital, with gleaming skyscrapers rising up in the middle of nowhere. This was rather different.

As evening approached, Madame peered out at a hundred empty chairs set before the stage and turned to Freddie, our tour manager. She asked him, in the coaxing way she did whenever she encountered an obstacle: 'Dear, do you believe we will have an audience? From where will it come?'

Madame always spoke English with elegance and formality, but her German grammar sounded to our ears as though her sentences were back to front.

'Don't worry, Madame,' he replied. His voice was bright, although his expression was doubtful. He assured us that an audience of cultured government officials would materialise.

'If people do not come, we will regard this as a rehearsal,' said Madame. 'And Frau Gertie will correct more mistakes.'

Madame often referred to herself in the third person, and as 'Frau Gertie' when she had to put up with inconveniences.

Madame accepted everything about these Australian tours stoically. She was something of an anomaly, this small, sophisticated artist in her stylish little black hat, looking out of place in the Australian countryside. But she persevered and ignored little hardships we encountered with unshakeable optimism. No matter the obstacle, she was always polite and good natured.

And, sure enough, Freddie had been right: at eight o'clock that night, every one of those hundred seats was full, and it was one of the most appreciative audiences of that tour.

After we performed, bowed, packed and dressed, we would then attend the reception put on by the local people. Most towns would host a reception, and they were greatly appreciated by every one of us. If the locals had simply applauded and gone away, our tours would have been lonely affairs.

In Canberra, our hosts had set up a buffet table loaded with warm sausage rolls, chocolate logs, cream sponges and lamingtons. We gazed longingly at the feast, but we had standing orders from Madame to never eat more than one, small, plain cake, with no cream. 'I forbid you girls to get fat!'

The prohibition was terrible for a hungry young woman who had just danced her heart out and could hear her stomach rumbling. I had a special desire for the lamingtons – a square of sponge cake, dipped in thick chocolate sauce or icing, and rolled in grated coconut, found only in Australia.

I once heard of a meeting of Australian war brides in America. They wept when they entered the room and saw plates full of lamingtons that had been prepared especially for them. After touring Australia on an empty stomach, I believe that story.

However, in Canberra, we had not been forbidden the sausage rolls, and we helped ourselves to several of those. Then, eating as daintily as possible with a coffee in one hand and a heaped plate in the other, we mingled with the locals and accepted compliments on behalf of the company.

In some Australian country towns we stayed in homes, but often we went to one of the typical country hotels that could be seen on almost every corner. Many more people than we could imagine must have passed through these towns. We never performed on Saturdays because no one would come to see us. On Saturday, men went to the pubs and listened to the races being broadcast on the radio. The sound of the race broadcast came right into our rooms, accompanied by the smell of beer.

Regardless of the atmosphere, we would put on our finest show, and once our bows were over, Madame would hurry onto the stage wearing a dramatic coat I'd made especially for her, and with artful little steps she'd propel herself right up to the footlights. There, teetering on the edge of the darkness beyond, she would make her speech: 'Vee are so happy to have been able to come to zis charming town of Tumbulgum (or Dusty Hill, or Sheep Dip Gully, or whatever far-flung place we were in), and vee shall take with us ze happiest memories, of ze most hospitable people vee could have ze pleasure to know.'

We dancers, who had difficulty remembering the names of the towns we passed through, always wondered if Madame, with her eccentric English, would flounder and forget what she had to say. She never did. Not once.

༄

Very little could dent Madame's spirit. The only time I saw her truly upset was when Evelyn and Bettina – her star dancers, who had accompanied her since before the war – decided to go back to Vienna. She was left with only Emmy and Shona and her Australian students.

None of us could do what Evelyn and Bettina could. Their departure made it impossible for Madame to stage some of her best-loved works, and I missed them dearly.

Madame 'saw black', meaning she was devastated and downcast, but only for a little while. A creative artist never sees black for very long. She choreographed dances tailored to each of us, like 'Wheel of Life' for Coralie Hinkley, Mardi Watchorn and me. She taught us some of her beautiful earlier dances, sometimes called 'vignettes' – short group dances such as 'I and Thou', 'Cart Drawn by Men' and others – which required a special kind of technique and feeling for sculptural forms.

Gradually, with the help of Emmy, who remembered every dance Madame had choreographed, she rebuilt her group to its original high standard.

The famous 'Waterlilies' was one of these earlier works she taught to her Australian dancers. 'Waterlilies' is a dance that seems very simple but is very exact in its movements. Although short, it was always very successful.

First, the hands cover the face, and the movement is created mainly by the breath. The breath affects the whole body, so the hands over the face do not actually move except for what the breath does to them.

The second breath, both hands move slightly, but without revealing the face or the eyes.

With intake of the third breath, the hands move to the right, palms facing up; and the head leans sideways, to seem as if lying on the upturned palms.

The hands have hardly enough time to go back to the beginning before the movement starts again, covering the eyes.

Then the hands are slowly lowered, and continue down, suggestively coming to rest on the chest. Yet it is not at all sexy, with Madame's good taste and her awareness of deeper shades of meaning.

All through this dance, we were taught that we must be aware of our breathing. It helps create emotion and the right amount of drama.

After a slight pause, the next part begins, with full arm curves, right arm, left arm and so on. There is an unexpected move, when both arms of the two girls come over in a slightly surprising togetherness – then back to one arm, then the other. The hands rest on the chest for about three beats, waiting for the next musical notes to come, compelling the arms. Then together they move upwards – instead of bending sideways as they had been.

This kind of unexpected shift was something Madame often did. It lifted a movement briefly into a new realm, making a world of difference. Another example I remember was when two dancers in Strauss's

'The Blue Danube' were crossing the stage fairly close to each other. At a certain moment, one girl's arm slipped across the other girl's back in a gesture of humanity and friendliness – a moment of connection. Madame was full of such natural yet fanciful loveliness. She was not of the somewhat grim school of Germanic modern dance.

In 'Waterlilies', the movement of the arms in and out, gliding forward and back to the chest, takes place with a few variations, until it ends with hands closed into fists and winding about each other – 'like tendrils,' as Madame said.

The last sequence involves straightening the body, arms out on both sides. Slowly the arms close about the body, finally coming to rest.

I have had many partners in this dance over the years. I have been in the front, or the back, depending entirely on who was taller or shorter. The last was my close friend Jean (Poppy) Raymond. Each evening as we left the stage I would complain because Jean angled her arms instead of gracefully curving them as I thought she should. She was not impressed with my critique and continued to angle each time.

'Waterlilies' suited my strengths as a dancer. I was not the most technically gifted, and not capable of the astonishing leaps or sheer magnetism that the Austrian girls had brought to the company, but I felt very deeply. Madame saw this and knew that 'Waterlilies' was for me.

There were those among us who were capable of more vigorous movement, so they learned exciting dances like 'The Slavonic Dance' and 'The Demon Machine'. This last had been choreographed in Vienna quite early in Madame's career and had created a sensation at the time. It still caused a sensation every time we performed it. I loved to be part of that dance – even if I had a very small role – just a piston in a diabolical machine that drew in the innocent dancers to corrupt them.

By the end of each tour we were tired, but it was a wonderful kind of tiredness, following a period of hard, satisfying work – with generous audiences, fine scenery and lots of silly fun. We delighted in meeting people, knowing we had pleased them, and sharing in Madame's purpose of bringing joy and wonder to the world through her dance.

As well as our successful domestic tours, Madame also began to take our group overseas. Under her wing, we had the most amazing adventures and saw corners of the world none of us ever expected to. We toured South Africa and what was then called Rhodesia, and found ourselves confronted by the stark hardship and prejudice of societies there.

Another tour took us by steamship to New Zealand, and a successful season in Christchurch. We had full houses, and newspapers were full of praise.

In one newspaper was a two-panel cartoon showing a man being led reluctantly through the doorway into the theatre by his wife. And in the second panel he is seen flying out onto the street from the theatre in a typical expansive Bodenwieser high leap. The caption read, 'My wife drags me to these things. I don't understand ballet, but I understand this!'

A simple review, perhaps, but a true one. For all the high-minded philosophy and theory behind the Bodenwieser technique, the dances were understandable by anyone. They were pure expressions of emotion and grace and could slip past cultural barriers – from Tumbulgum to Cape Town. Which is, I think, one of the finest things an artist can do through their work.

Chapter Six

Gateway to India / Colour and Movement

AFTER OUR INTERNATIONAL TOUR, WE SOON returned to our normal way of life with regular classes, until news came that we had an offer to go to India for quite a long season in the autumn of 1952. We were thrilled by the prospect.

Soon after we heard this news, I happened to be walking along Pitt Street with Basil Pattison, Bodenwieser's only male dancer, and passed the movie house where a short documentary about India was screening.

On impulse we bought tickets and took our seats in the theatre. On the screen we saw beautiful Hindu girls in richly coloured saris walking through a temple in Benares. A holy man, wearing nothing except for a few leaves that seemed to have stuck to his skin, sat on a bank at the side of the road and looked as if he were made of the same earth on which he sat. In a wide-open space in New Delhi we saw a lively, noisy colourful religious procession. The scene changed – racing across the Gobi Desert to a remote temple where students were learning to do exercises that would help them on their spiritual journeys.

We saw a girl receiving dance instruction. It was a form of movement intended to unite the dancer with the world spirit.

'That's where we'll be soon,' Basil whispered in the semi-darkness.

'I know,' I whispered back. We were awed, but also excited.

We were to leave for India in less than a month.

⁓

We travelled by ship as usual. This time it was a large passenger liner, unlike the two cargo ships we had travelled on previously.

As the ship approached Bombay, I became aware of a unique odour wafting across the bay from the city. It was the scent of spices, garbage and jasmine flowers. No one else seemed to notice it. To me it said, 'Here is India.' I found it exhilarating.

When the ship docked, we were looked after by an agent of the Taj Hotel and taken directly to that famous old building overlooking the Gateway to India, a huge stone arch under which the British traditionally passed when formally entering or leaving India. Years earlier they had made their last formal departure under this archway. All sorts of people now passed under the Gateway to India. As for the Taj Hotel, it was the last word in splendour – a long white palace of a hotel on the very edge of the bay. We were to be treated to two nights in luxury to acclimatise before beginning our tour – first stop Calcutta.

It was like being in a dream. We wandered through marble halls and up a grand, spiralling staircase. Everywhere was the scent of sandalwood. Silent young men moved about noiselessly, ready to serve us should we need them.

Jean and I were given a large room with a balcony and views across the Gateway to India and the bay. After we had settled in, the bearer served us high tea on the veranda. This was a luxury, but we soon found out we were expected to share it with the local wildlife. As I was about to put a piece of cake into my mouth, a bold black raven flew between my fork and my mouth and skilfully took it from me. I was shocked, but then I didn't mind at all. It was part of India. My lips were brushed by a raven's wing. How thrilling!

From Bombay we travelled to Calcutta, where we were met by a jolly group of young European men. They bustled us into cars and took us to our hotel – a very grand one overlooking the Maidan, a wide park, where festivals and processions often took place.

The hotel had its own concert hall with a stage and lights. This was where we were to perform. We were to give both solo and group dances. With Madame, we made arrangements for rehearsals the next day and our first performance the following night.

Before the first show began, we looked through a peephole and saw an audience of well-dressed people who had come to see the Viennese Modern Company, as we were called in India. The local women always looked as if they were in evening dress, elegant in saris and jewellery. They were so impressive that even the Europeans, who may not always bother to dress up, were encouraged to make the best of themselves.

It was a hot night. The men wore tropical suits with white shoes, and they looked cooler than I felt. They must have been. I could scarcely remember being so hot in my life.

We had great difficulty in changing costumes. They were wet with our own sweat and stuck to our skin. Basil had to work hard between scenes, helping us with our changes. He had several dances to perform himself, and he too struggled, so we in turn helped him.

One of our group dances was the 'Austrian Peasant Dance', which includes the famous leg-slapping sequence. Basil did this very well – hopping, lifting each leg in turn, slapping the thigh, the calf and the foot. Moira Claux, Tania Butler and Margaret Frazer also took the part of thigh-slapping boys; Jean and I were girls.

For the round dance, in which we turned under our partner's arm while moving around in the circle, I was able to spin like a top under Moira's arm, for turning fast was a thing I could do very well.

Of course, we also performed 'The Blue Danube' waltz, 'Waterlilies' and some new solo dances that Madame had choreographed for this tour. Our efforts were rewarded with rousing applause. The Europeans in the audience found the peasant dance curiously nostalgic, while the Indians considered it the height of exoticism.

Nights were for performance. We were free in the daytime. I liked walking about observing the people. Everywhere, pagodas and arches had a greyish-greenish tinge. All the buildings looked to me like crumbling old ruins – but they weren't. They were quite solid – just painted over with mould from the monsoon.

One day we were in the Maidan having publicity photos taken, when suddenly the skies opened up and we found ourselves standing in a four-inch flood. We sheltered in vain under an archway for a while before conceding defeat, removing our shoes, and walking back through the flood to our hotel.

For two months we lived and performed in Calcutta, in heat so oppressive that ice-cream – by the time it travelled from the kitchen to the hotel dining room – would melt all over the plate. We Australians, who had thought ourselves well-built for heat, wilted in a similar way after two months.

Towards the end of the tour, we found ourselves in the midst of a riot – or rather, looking out at one from the stone balcony of the hotel. Below us, a crowd of young men rushed about with police in hot pursuit, brandishing short black sticks. One young man stood before a policeman with his hands held together before his chest in a sort of pleading gesture. The policeman's answer was a bang on the head with a short black stick. All the policemen had these sticks, and were hitting any of the men they could catch.

Madame put her head around the doorway from the corridor inside. 'Girls, girls. Come away. It will all be over in a little while.'

The crowd was dispersing. The worst seemed to be over. Madame was unfazed. She was European and had seen riots and disturbances.

'Ah, you girls have never seen revolution. That is what the Tsar of Russia said before they cut off his head.'

We were not sure of the historical accuracy of this statement, but we respected Madame's point of view. She was, by far, the worldliest of us all, and our journey was set to continue.

⁂

We left Calcutta by plane late that afternoon and reached New Delhi after dark. This meant we weren't able to see very much of the ancient, sprawling city.

However, the first glimpse of our hotel pleased us. It stood in its own grounds and looked as if it would have luxurious rooms. We were given double rooms opening onto a long veranda where delightful, tame little squirrel-like animals nested in a rich green vine. Madame was given the grandest room of all, but we thought that was right and proper.

We had dinner and then returned to our rooms to sleep. Like the hotel in Calcutta, this one had its own performance space, and this was where we were to rehearse the next morning.

I wished we didn't have to have a rehearsal, for I wanted to go out immediately and see this historical city and its surroundings. I had a great interest in Indian history, and especially the Mughal Empire – times of great change and bloodshed that made India one of the wealthiest, most influential, powerful, intellectual and spiritual countries on Earth.

This interest was shared by a man I was destined to meet at a reception held for us by the Australian Consulate.

André Moitessier was a Frenchman, working in Delhi for the Commercial Consul. At the reception itself I hardly spoke to him, but when it was time to leave, he offered to drive us back to our accommodation. Instead of taking us directly to our hotel, this lover of Mughal art took us to his room in another hotel near ours. Shortly afterwards, some of the other guests from the Consulate arrived and the party continued. We drank champagne and laughed a lot and left at about midnight.

As we were leaving, we passed through a small room on our way to the door. I stopped to look at our host's collection of original Mughal paintings. As I looked, with some little exclamations of delight, I became aware that André was standing close beside me.

He seemed pleased by my pleasure and what little knowledge I had of the paintings. I knew something about them because I had drawn on various styles of Indian art when designing costumes for our dance 'O World'. I told him about my discoveries, and he seemed fascinated. The feeling was mutual.

He confessed that he had seen me dance when he had visited Calcutta recently. The champagne supper had been planned so that we could meet like this. I was touched and intrigued. As soon as we had settled into our routine here in New Delhi, André devoted himself to me, and to revealing to me the treasures of the ancient Delhi and the great Mughal buildings.

André told me of an ancient pleasure pool of one of the emperors that lay to the north. He offered to drive me to see it. To reach the pool, which sat alone in the middle of a plain edged by ruins of a past Delhi, we had to leave the road and pass through a medieval village where the people lived quietly away from the outside world.

The pool was a large square tank still holding water from rain. Around the edge on three sides were arched walls. On the fourth side was a majestic flight of steps leading from the ground level down to the pool itself. Another narrow staircase cut into one of the walls led to the roof. We sat up there and watched peacocks on one of the distant ramparts.

As the sun was setting, they opened their tails and posed like proud kings. On the other side of the plain, we saw the silhouettes of large cat-like animals posing with the same pride on the roof of a ruined palace. From below came the tinkling laughter of village children who had come to splash about in the stagnant water of the emperor's pool.

After several romantic excursions such as this one, I could think of little else but André.

I managed to dance properly, and I hoped Madame wasn't aware of how much time I spent with my new French lover. She preferred us not to show interest in romantic entanglements on tour – the danger was that we would abandon her in pursuit of new passion. If we absolutely had to, she encouraged us to leave romance in the rear-view mirror once it was done: 'Zee woman on the spot gets zee man!' she would tell us. 'Not those passing through.'

Still, I hoped she never needed me for anything during the daytime for I was often in his room. I spent time there even while he was in his office. One weekend, when we were free, André invited Jean and Basil to accompany us to Agra and see the Taj Mahal – one of the greatest monuments to undying love the world has ever known.

The sun was low when we reached Agra. We saw the garden and the tomb and the long stretch of pool water in the soft afternoon light. As the sun continued to lower, sunset pink was reflected by the water and caught by the luminous pearl of the dome.

Across the river, the towers and domes of the palace within the walls of the fort were a deep purple-red against the darkening sky.

After a while, Jean and Basil went to wait in the car. André and I sat romancing in the garden until it grew dark. Fireflies turned themselves into brilliant little flashes of light among the trees and reflected in the water all about us.

On one or two occasions like this, I had caught André watching me as though he were living through the afternoon via my emotions and reactions, with none of his own.

With a sort of amused regret, he seemed to appreciate my joy vicariously – as though through me he was experiencing things anew for the first time. It didn't bother me; nothing could spoil the rapture I was living with. No warning signs disturbed me, if warnings they were.

When the time came for the Bodenwieser dancers to depart Delhi, we threw a party. I dressed myself in a rich rose-coloured sari André had bought for me, and with Jean and André's friend, Rudy, we went to one of the other luxurious hotels in New Delhi for the farewell dinner.

There was so much fun and feverish excitement that there was no thought of parting. When dinner was over, André and Rudy waited while Jean and I changed our clothes, as brides do when they are leaving for the honeymoon, and then they took us to the airport. There we met the rest of the company, without Madame. For some reason I was unaware of, she had gone ahead of us to Bombay.

I don't know what she would have thought of the final farewell that took place at the airport, with the rest of the company and the boyfriends and admirers who had come to see us off.

We took charge of the whole airport waiting room, and only when it was time to board the plane did I fully realise that I was leaving André.

Four years were to pass before I saw him again.

Our plane took us to Bombay, where we spent two more days and nights at the Taj waiting for the ship that was to take us back to Australia.

Madame's great worry about taking her dancers on international tours was that she would lose us to the allure of the road. There were two great dangers. One, that we would fall in love and follow our suitor across the world. The other was that we would fall in love with travel itself and leave behind the disciplined life of the modernist dancer in favour of a more adventurous, free-spirited existence.

I was not immune to either of these temptations.

Chapter Seven

Bombay / The Big Picture

About twelve months after our India tour, in 1953, I told Madame I wanted to leave her. I said I wanted to study the great art works of Italy. The galleries of masterpieces, the ancient frescoes. This was true, but it was not my only reason for leaving. The truth was that Madame was creating ever more ambitious work, and she needed stronger dancers than myself to realise them.

That was how I felt at the time, in any case. I was very conscious of my limited technique, and I was afraid Madame would lose interest in me. I was insecure, and perhaps paranoid; my fears may have been groundless.

Madame had chosen me as a dancer for my soft, expressive qualities, not my technical mastery. She may not have wanted anything more than that – anything more than me – but I didn't give either of us an opening to talk about it. This was a failing of mine – not being able to talk about what was troubling me. I ran away instead.

I travelled with Margaret Frazer – another Bodenwieser dancer who had fallen in love in India. The ship would dock in Bombay en route to Europe, she would depart, and I would travel on to Italy to wander alone around art museums. However, just before we sailed, I changed my mind and decided to leave the ship with Margaret, following my heart and abandoning my European plans, for India.

When we finally docked in Bombay, we collected our luggage and went straight to the only hotel we knew, the Taj. We shared a room, had dinner in the grand dining room, sat around in the huge lounge and then went to bed. Next morning, Margaret left for Calcutta where her Englishman waited to take her to the altar. She looked a little lost as we said goodbye, but I expected she would soon be in the arms of her man and happy ever after.

Left to myself, I sat around again in the luxury of the Taj and wondered what to do next. I did not have to wonder for more than half a day. I phoned some people I knew who fixed me up as a lodger with a local woman. Her name was Lena. She was a sweet, sober lady who tried in earnest to teach me how to make dishes in the Indian method, using a pressure cooker – a process that often involved me diving behind a doorframe expecting the device to explode like a grenade. That turned out to be sufficiently trying for both of us, and soon we were bonded by the shared trauma. I became almost a member of her family.

Through my Australian friends in Bombay I met Laura Hamilton, a professional singer. I asked her to study some English and American folk songs with me, and our rehearsals soon took me straight back to the Taj Hotel.

Laura's dear friend was Darob Tata, the managing director of the hotel. The Taj was a stately establishment left over from the days of British rule. Darob, a youthful 40-year-old from a wealthy industrial family in India, had come into ownership of the hotel, and the grand old place had become his private playground. He had a suite of rooms with a piano on the top floor and plenty of space, so we rehearsed our folk songs up there.

Darob took an interest in what we were doing and suggested we perform in the supper room for the hotel guests – frequently English and Anglophile Indians who longed to hear old-fashioned folk music.

Ours was an informal arrangement, but Darob – being a generous and open sort of man – invited me to stay at the Taj while Laura and I were working together. It was time for me to leave Lena's apartment anyway, as her husband had returned and there wasn't much room for me anymore, so I gladly accepted Darob's invitation.

I made costumes, masks and set decorations for our performance. Laura stood under a folksy apple tree I'd made and sang the songs, while I danced or mimed in a red cotton dress I'd made from hand-loomed fabric of the sort that was a symbol of India's resilience and pride in its weaving industry.

I stayed another four months at the Taj, dancing at night and exploring Bombay by day. Laura was often away on long singing engagements in Delhi, Lahore or Calcutta, but when she was in residence, we would work on new songs together. I believe she was in love with Darob. He and I had become friends, nothing more, and she thankfully had no qualms about leaving me with him. I hadn't forgotten André and felt his absence very often. I imagined him walking the forlorn streets of Paris, looking for me while I searched for him in the sultry heat of Bombay.

I was startled one afternoon, lying in the heat, trying to sleep, when I became aware of half-naked young men climbing about outside on the stone balustrade; some even appeared to be hanging almost upside down from the balcony above.

I hurried downstairs and out to the street to investigate. With my back to the Bay of Bombay and my neck craned up to take in the hotel facade, I saw dozens of young men scaling the Taj, dragging long black electrical cords with them.

They were not a swarm of robbers, merely covering the walls of the Taj with festive lights for the hotel's upcoming birthday celebrations that would take place in a week's time. The Taj was going to be lit up, every inch of it. My balcony alone had lights every two feet across it. When they were finally switched on, it was a sight to behold.

One night before the lights were due to taken down, I had dinner in the dining room with Darob, where I wondered out loud what it would be like to see the lights from a distance: 'I wish we could take a boat and row right out to the middle of the bay.'

It was just an idea, but to my surprise Darob replied, 'We could. I have a boat – just a small one. It's a calm night. No trouble at all.'

He instructed the chief electrician not to turn off the lights at eleven o'clock, which was when they were scheduled to be switched off, but to leave them on until twelve. He was the director of the hotel after all and could do as he liked.

At about eleven o'clock, we went down to the stone jetty and boarded Darob's small rowing boat. Darob took the oars facing away from the shore because I said we mustn't look until we were far out in the middle of the bay. I too sat with my back to the shore. It was a calm, warm night, hazy but clear enough to see our way. The surface of the water was like silk. There were few other vessels in our way once we were far enough out. I felt no fear at all of being in such a tiny boat with water fathoms deep beneath us. Apart from the faint sound of the oars dipping into the water, there was a magical silence.

In the distance behind us, the Taj Hotel, glowing in its festive, electrical costume, dominated its end of the shoreline. We waited until the anticipation was unbearable, then I cried, 'Now!'

As one we turned to take in the view, and in that moment, the electricity went out! The great bulk of the Taj loomed only as a dark shape, like a castle against a darker sky. We were disappointed and for a few moments Darob was angry. But we accepted our loss fatalistically. I don't remember ever mentioning it again. It would have been lovely to see the Taj all lit up, but the night and the strange quietness of our voices had been quite enchanting, so we didn't mind much.

I loved Bombay, or Bom Bahia, or Mumbai, or whatever else it has been called in the mists of its past. I found it to be about the most fascinating and interesting city I have ever been to. It's like a vast carpet with all the living patterns of India woven into it.

For centuries it has welcomed anyone who wished to trade and allowed them to get their feet in until they thought they owned the place. All those characters: Portuguese, Dutch, Parsees, Turks, ancient Greeks, the British and the Americans, dogs, cats, monkeys, cows, snakes and ravens, beggars, orphans, Bharatanatyam dancers and holy men, film stars, money lenders, Catholic nuns, priests, bottlewallas and hotel managers. They're all in the carpet too. And now, I felt, so was I.

As time passed, I became fascinated by the Ellora Caves, a unique artistic creation that I felt embodied this great 'spiritual carpet'. It was a complex of thirty-four monasteries and temples that, over hundreds of years, had been devoted in different ages to Buddhism, Hinduism and Jainism.

It was first brought to Western attention by a young officer during the British Raj, who had made the journey by horseback and written a terribly romantic book about it called *The Wonders of Elora*. This book inspired me to make my own journey, which I would also have liked to make by horseback, but had to settle for the modern method, by car, with a group of friends.

As we drove across the plain, we could see what looked like a string of dark holes along the base of the scarp of a long wide plateau. Then, as we got closer, we saw that around the edge the rock had been carved and sculpted so that each hole seemed to have jewels around it.

When we reached the first of the caves and the car was brought to a standstill, we sensed the eerie loneliness and deathlike silence of the place. This was pre-Mughal India, a colossal work of art from a cultural age that existed long before the first Mohammedans came down from the north in 664.

We parked the car and walked up to the caves, which we entered one after the other. We marvelled at the artistry of the sculptor-monks who had carved and chiselled and hacked at the stone over such a long time. The religion changed, and back again, but the devotion persevered, like the river that ran through the cave complex and served those holy men. I thought it was wonderful that we could still hear it.

Before we left Ellora we entered one more cave, where we found a thin wall that had been broken through by ancient tools. It was large enough for us to pass through to an unexpected narrow ledge overlooking a gully, hidden from the outside plain. Making our way around the rock ledge we came to a delightful little waterfall. Hidden as it was from all except the sky, it was as if we had been transported by the genie of Aladdin's lamp to this cool place within a mountain. As we bathed our arms, legs and faces, we reflected on the monks who must have refreshed themselves here for century upon century.

⁓

While I danced for room and board at the Taj, I drew no wages. A curious life: I lived in luxury, but had no money of my own. My mother wrote, telling me she had sent some via a bank in the city, but it had never reached me. Before long, my resources ran out completely.

I had one rupee left and didn't know what I should do with it. I envisioned myself in a saffron robe, beggars' cup in hand, walking towards the Himalayas and never being heard of again. Since landing in India, I had immersed myself in the study of Buddhist and Hindu philosophy, but there was a limit to how far I could go on 'the middle way' – the Buddhist teaching of avoiding extravagance – not caring about money. Yet I had never thought of asking for it at the Taj until now.

A few days later, with a hundred repetitive thoughts about ridiculous solutions to the problem of being alive, I sat on my balcony having tea. Across the bay, just visible through the haze, was the island of Elephanta, an ancient temple complex in a series of caves. It featured a Trimurti – a statue of Shiva depicting all three of his aspects: creator, protector, destroyer – that was rumoured to be a masterwork of art. I longed to see it but had never found the opportunity.

Looking down to the harbour, I saw a small boat moored at the stone jetty and called out to the boatman, asking if he could take me to Elephanta for one rupee. To my surprise, he said yes. 'It is a long way, memsahib. We must leave now.'

I was ready and off we went. I sat on a wooden board facing the boatman, while his 'crew' sat behind me with nothing much to do. The single sail was not unfurled, as there was no wind that day. The boy sitting behind me must have been about ten years old. A single rupee, I told myself, was not really enough for an afternoon's work, yet none of them seemed at all concerned about that. They had agreed to the deal and made no complaints.

It was calm and dreamy in the Bay of Bombay. I became conscious of the sound of the oars as the boatman moved them through the water. It was a lovely gentle rhythm, like a lullaby. Hours must have passed like that as the little waves lapped against the side of the boat.

'When will we get there?' I asked, not actually out of impatience, but simple curiosity. It did seem to be a long way.

'In a minute, memsahib. In a minute,' the boatman replied so soothingly that I could have fallen asleep. His minute passed, and another, until three hours had gone by. I didn't mind at all.

At last we reached the wooden jetty, jutting out from the rocky shore of the island. I stepped onto it in a dreamy, unguarded state and walked up the path towards the entrance to the cave, and the Trimurti.

The three faces of Shiva on Elephanta rise from a base, wider than it is deep. There are actually five heads in total, but only three are visible. The fourth head is hidden within the rock wall behind the first three faces. The fifth, which is invisible, will never be seen. This face represents the last mystery that exists in the creation of the universe.

I walked slowly through the semi-darkness towards the three enormous faces of Shiva – one front face and two profiles. I stood there utterly captivated by their splendour and beauty. The stone cheeks, the half-closed eyelids and the full, sensuous lips all seemed to have the glow of living flesh. The ornaments on their heads were like real jewels.

Everything about them was gentle and calm, great, and strong. As I gazed at them, something happened. The walls of the cave rolled away. I was left standing where I was, only now in a wide-open space. The three faces had moved apart, becoming three separate colossal masses of natural rock.

I felt objects – tiny physical things – like nuts and bolts dropping out of my head onto the floor and going *plonk, plonk, plonk* and then rolling away. And I heard a voice say, 'You have been looking at life in petty fragments instead of great sculptural forms.'

Time, of course, does not usually exist when something like this takes place, so I don't know how long I stood there. I was drawn back into the stream of time by the voice of the boatman, urging me back. We had begun our journey back to Bombay.

That night in the hotel, I tried to convey my experience to a guest of the hotel – a sophisticated American woman, slick and smart, with a silver streak of hair and lots of mascara. She told me, 'Oh, my dear Miss Kramer. You sound like a woman who has found peace.'

I realised I needed to take the long view – worry less about the smaller things. I've always remembered that epiphany, and it has stood me in good stead. I no longer carry on repetitive dialogues with my troublesome self late at night.

My mother's money turned up, in what I considered a very Indian sort of way.

A strange man came to see me at the hotel.

'Hello,' he said. 'Why have you not come to get your money?'

'My money?'

He explained that he was an employee of a bank, far away on the other side of Bombay. Apparently, the money my mother had sent had been waiting for me for some time. They had no idea where to send it until a curious bank employee told a cousin, who told a friend, who told a second cousin, and so on and so forth, until the mystery was solved. The money was for 'the Australian girl who dances at the Taj'.

That was the way I came to know how my banking business was being conducted in Bombay.

Shortly after that, Darob must have realised that I had never received any money for my folk songs, and suddenly I was paid. It was often the way – once I had resolved to try and see life in its broad, sculptural shapes, then my problems would seem to resolve themselves.

Now that I'd had two unexpected windfalls, I decided to move on. After an excitable farewell with all the friends I had made in Bombay, I purchased a train ticket for New Delhi.

Chapter Eight

No Fixed Abode / India Bag

When the train reached New Delhi, I went straight to the YWCA where I booked a room in a long narrow dormitory – one of many separated by green lawns with peacocks and peahens strolling around. On my first night I made friends with a Hindu girl, and we dragged our cots out onto the lawn to sleep under the stars and wake up among the peacocks.

One of the permanent residents at the YWCA was an English woman named Penny, who – when I showed photographs of my work with English and American folk songs – insisted on taking me to meet the Mother Superior of the convent in New Delhi.

'They are so proud of their new auditorium. I'm sure they'd be glad to have you perform there. It has wonderful acoustics. They say you can hear a pin drop in the back row.'

Penny was to be my spokeswoman, my manager and agent. She introduced me to an Anglo-Indian girl who played piano and was eager to be my accompanist. I intended to be both singer and dancer, as I didn't have a singer to work with me in New Delhi, so I would perform both roles myself.

I meekly allowed Penny to carry me off in her car to meet the Irish Mother Superior. I didn't have to say anything. My new friend told her about my folk songs, suggesting how nice it would be to have the pupils see me perform.

'Reverend Mother, you haven't really used the new auditorium. Here is an opportunity,' said Penny.

'But Penny,' Mother Superior replied in a strong Irish accent, 'we are so busy getting ready for exams. I don't think so. No, I'm afraid not, dear.'

Penny snatched one of the photographs I held in my hands. 'Look, Mother. Molly Malone and all that.'

I was surprised to see the imposing Mother yield. Her cheeks flushed with colour like a young girl in love.

'Ah,' she sighed. 'Molly Malone.'

In showing her a picture of me in my red costume and green apron, pushing an imaginary wheelbarrow through the streets of Dublin crying, 'Cockles and mussels, alive, alive, oh,' Penny had played her trump card. The Mother Superior was lonely for Ireland, so

I was allowed to perform for the whole school, and each student was to pay a few coins.

On the afternoon of my concert, I stood on the stage of the convent's fine new auditorium and looked down at the rows of schoolgirls with their neat uniforms. How strange to be on stage as a singer again, in a school, all those years after leaving the Conservatorium. It was a nice feeling and, as I began to sing, I could hear by the sound of the piano and my own voice that Penny had been right about the auditorium's acoustics.

When it was over, I stayed on stage signing my name in dozens of autograph books thrust at me. When there were no more to sign, I followed a young nun, who had stayed to keep me company, to the room where a sweet-faced Indian nun made a fresh pot of tea. The Mother Superior looked pleased and handed me a purse with all the money the children had paid.

I had not expected to debut in Delhi as a singer of folk songs, but I was pleased I did. Although New Delhi is one of the largest cities in the world – even then – word of mouth spread and reached the ears of hoteliers. Shortly after that, I left the YWCA and went to another of New Delhi's leading hotels where I got a contract to dance and sing Western songs in the supper room.

I was given the 'Roof Garden' suite on the top floor of the hotel's annex, a few minutes' walk from the main hotel building. I was only mildly disappointed to find this name was overly ambitious; there was no garden on the roof at all, but it did overlook a lush green expanse that flushed golden at the end of the day. I took private delight in my pre-show ritual, walking out to my 'roof garden' to watch the sunset.

When my contract came to an end in New Delhi, I was able to get an engagement at the Metropole Hotel in Karachi, Pakistan. I was very pleased that word of my talents had reached across the border as far away as Karachi. It was only after I'd made the journey and set up in the Metropole as a dancer that I realised someone had told the hotel manager that my talents included painting.

I was somewhat surprised when, the morning after I arrived, the manager led me across a dewy lawn to a pavilion opening onto the hotel garden. With a grand gesture that indicated all three walls, he said, 'Do you think you could paint something nice for the guests to look at while they have dinner?'

It was a wide building, open on one side, which served as dance floor, concert hall or simply as bandstand. Sitting in the garden on summer nights, hotel guests would be able to see the whole of the inside of this building.

The tables were set out on the lawn facing it and the garden was lit with festive lights. It was a lovely space, and if the manager had hired me on recommendation as a painter, who was I to argue?

He wanted 'something nice' so I felt that gave me freedom to paint anything I liked, provided it wasn't offensive to local custom. So I said yes. I gave a list of the colours and the brush sizes required, and also requested an assistant, a ladder, buckets for water and lots of rags for wiping. As I wrote my list, I began to envision what I would do.

The work would be called 'Scenes of Paris'. The theme was a simple one. Two art students, a boy and a girl, with a somewhat childlike, cartoonish appearance, were to make their way to various well-known locations in Paris – a sort of artistic tour of Paris for hotel guests who were either homesick for France or could not travel there themselves. One thing I had surmised correctly – the cosmopolitan and educated Pakistanis longed to see Paris as much as anyone else in the world with a romantic streak. I described my idea to the hotel manager, who was enthusiastic.

By the next morning, not one, but two assistants were already at work, stretching coarse cotton fabric onto wooden frames that they attached to the walls. While they worked, I found the hotel band and we rehearsed my dances for that evening. When the rehearsal was over, I returned to the pavilion and found the two young boys waiting for me. The walls were ready for my 'Scenes of Paris'.

If I'd had the time to think about it, I would have perhaps not even attempted the task. I would have said, 'This is a project for an artist who has been trained to paint murals.' As it was, I had no time for self-doubt or second guessing. After all – I had made careful study of great works of art in every city I had visited. I had spent time with painters, and modelled for them, and seen the way an artwork takes shape. Why shouldn't I paint my mural of Paris in Karachi?

All things considered, I was very pleased with the outcome. The manager was as well, and we received a strong reception from visitors to the hotel.

There was a great thirst for the exotic in India and Pakistan. The hotel regularly hired two Flamenco dancers, Marissa and Carmen. They were usually billed as Spanish, but when a South American band performed, they were billed as Brazilian. The summer season opened with a gala evening held in the garden, with dancing in the pavilion, and our 'Brazilian' dancers.

That night, during a social dance in the pavilion, there was a pause in the music. My dance partner, a hotel guest, asked the couple next to us how they liked the 'Scenes of Paris'.

'Oh,' replied the lady, 'aren't they lovely? I know the man who did them all!'

The music started up and we moved away. We thought it was funny and laughed about it. What can one do except laugh?

༄

I'd been at the Metropole for several months when a fascinating group of people came to the hotel. They were travelling through the East, collecting samples of folk music with battery-driven equipment. Leo was the leader, assisted by an American girl, Leslie, and a young Pakistani man, Rashid, who was acting as a guide.

They stayed for three weeks in the Metropole, and in that time, Leslie taught me some steps from a Turkish folk dance while Leo played his baglama, a Turkish string instrument. We put together a performance one night, in the hotel's supper room. I was so inspired by their musical power that when it was time for them to leave Karachi, I went with them.

We wandered and stopped in several villages where Leo made recordings of ancient, local folk music. On our journey, I encountered the most wonderful folk artists, sculptors and weavers. In these villages – as in the crowded marketplaces of Bombay and Delhi – I was sorely tempted by the riches of simple beauty. I had to restrain myself from purchasing bolts of fabric and trying to fit them into my luggage. In truth, I was already rather overburdened with costumes for dances I had added to my repertoire. Instead, I settled with filling up what I had taken to calling my 'India Bag' – a sort of mental rucksack in which I carefully stowed away my experiences. All that I was seeing, learning, feeling – I could carry an infinite amount in my India Bag.

We stopped at last in Lahore, a grand ancient city once known as 'the Paris of the East' because of its elegance and culture. There we met English and American members of a film company.

An actor from the company took us that night to what he called the 'Street of the Singing Girls'. It was not exactly a red-light district, but close to it.

The street was lined with small rooms on the ground level, with wide glass front walls so the interiors were quite visible. Each room was decorated and lit softly in a distinct colour – rose pink, sunset mauve, blue, sea green, exotic purple – and each was furnished with a couch of the same colour. Beautiful women veiled in silk in those colours reclined in languorous poses – alluring rather than 'sexy'. Outstretched arms undulated and with delicate wrist movements they beckoned to anyone who passed by.

I saw something there I'd not expected – the spirit body taking stage. As one of the beautiful, veiled women began to dance, I saw a change come over her. A moment before, she had been languid – a rather ribald sort of person – but as she began to dance, it was as if a goddess possessed her. In her confidence, in her grace, in the attention she brought to her expression, she became the dance.

I recognised in her an echo of what I felt when I was on stage. It's a kind of truth. You are one type of person before you step on stage, and then, while there, you become a manifestation of the dance. And when the music ends, you become yourself again. It's something I had experienced myself many times and had seen take place before my eyes, watching the great dancers of our age. I did not expect it here, in this dark dingy street, and for a moment I was far away, until a voice snapped me back to reality.

'Up here,' said our friend the actor. We climbed another staircase and entered a room that was all creamy white – from painted walls to pure, clean muslin-covered floor. White muslin-covered bolsters and cushions were stacked up along one wall for us to sit and lean on. The only colours in this room were the musical instruments held by four musicians seated on the floor at one end of the room, and in the exotic salwar kameez and veil of the singer seated in the middle. A dignified older woman in white, like the musicians, sat alone to the side. In a way she dominated the scene.

The actor whispered to us that she was the chaperone, there to see that everything was done properly; to negotiate should any rich man come seeking a mistress or a concubine, but not for one night's pleasure. The singer had her own ideas for her future. She wanted to be in movies and paid great attention to the actor and to Leo. She played her sitar and sang only for them, ignoring Leslie, Rashid and me. But after a while, realising she was not getting anywhere with them, she suddenly turned to Leslie and me and sang seductively, sitting directly in front of us and looking into our eyes as if to say, 'Use your influence for me.'

The actor had thought Leo might want to record the singer. 'She sings well and she's gorgeous,' Leo said, 'but I can buy that sort of music on tape.'

Rashid asked her to sing something else. But Leo still wasn't impressed. So after a while they gave some money to the chaperone, and we went away. I felt the singer's disappointment and was sorry for her.

*

We left Lahore the next day. We drove north, and late that afternoon we came to a place where four rivers met. We were too late to cross the bridge; it had been closed with a strong wooden gate, as it was every night, to prevent men from local tribes from coming over and making trouble with their rivals. The idea lent a slight air of danger to the crisp evening air.

There was no shelter, but the bank of the river was pleasant. We decided to stay there for the night. While we were choosing a place to make ourselves comfortable, we saw what looked like a mass of yellow moving towards us from a long way off on the road. As it came closer, we saw it was a group of people. The women, walking ahead of the men, wore voluminous yellow shawls over their heads. Their skirts, like huge black chrysanthemums, were similar to the skirts worn by the brick-carriers in New Delhi. Their earrings, nose rings and bangles glinted as they moved.

The men, very dashing with corkscrew curls, wore black Magyar coats over white blouses and putty-coloured pants. The coats were worn with one sleeve hanging loose so that it flew out when a gust of wind caught it. They carried their worldly possessions – rolled up rugs and cooking utensils – on their backs.

Settling down on the riverbank, they spread out their rugs and made themselves at home. Rashid understood what they were saying as he spoke several of the local languages and dialects. He went over to them and talked for a while. He came back and said we'd been invited to share their meal – simple chapattis as it turned out, with some rich sauce to flavour them.

Then we made preparations for a night by the river. Leslie and I were given the back of the van, while Leo and Rashid wrapped themselves in bedrolls on a grassy bank. The fire was alight for quite a long time, and we could hear the murmur of their voices, pleasant on the soft night air. We were not in the least afraid of these travellers. We slept soundly under the stars and woke in the morning to find they'd moved on.

⁓

I felt too, that it was time for me to move on. The time came for me to part from my companions – they went across the Khyber Pass to Afghanistan, and I back to Karachi.

The proprietor of a movie house next to the Metropole offered me a small part in a film he was producing. The role didn't require strong acting skills. I only had to learn some dance steps and the lines of a popular song in Urdu. I learned them so well that now, whenever I sing that song, I sing it in Urdu and have quite forgotten what the English words are.

With my mother and my brother Edward around 1917.

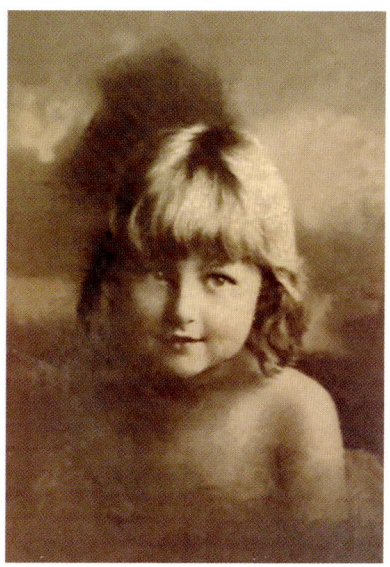

Me at three or four years old.

My father, mother and Edward in 1912. This is one of the few photos I have of my father.

In my Phillip Street days with Richard Want, my first love – and my former psychoanalyst!

Modelling a hat and coat I designed and made as part of a promotion for the Australian Wool Board, 1947.

Becoming part of the Bodenwieser company changed my life. The term 'Viennese Ballet' on our tour posters identified us as a modern dance company in the European expressive style.

Madame Gertrud Bodenwieser in the 1930s, before she was forced to flee Vienna in 1938.

National Library of Australia/Papers of Gertrud Bodenwieser

Madame with Emmy Taussig, one of her original Viennese dancers, judging a student examination in 1958. Modern expressive dance still required technique and discipline.

Left: My design for the costume I made for my first solo dance as a Bodenwieser student.
Right: Detail from Botticelli's *La Primavera*, which inspired my design.

Wikimedia Commons

Left: Dancing with Bodenwieser meant touring the world . . .

Above: Stepping out in Pietermaritzburg, South Africa, 1950. L–R: Margaret (Chappie) Chapple, Carol Huxtable, Elaine Vallance, Basil Pattison, me, Jean Raymond and Moira Claux.

Looking smart in Calcutta, India, 1952. L–R: Margaret Frazer, Jean Raymond, Basil Pattison, Moira Claux and Tania Butler. That's me in the front – naturally! Someone asked me at the time, 'Is that a hat or a veranda?'

Partying with hotel band members in Calcutta, 1952. Moira (centre) and me (behind).

A promotional portrait for Bodenwieser.

Dancing with Coralie Hinkley in 'O World'. I designed and made the costumes, using fabric enhanced with paint and embroidery.

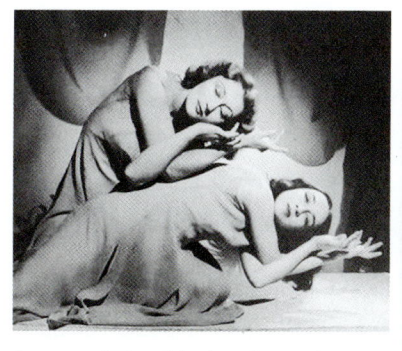

Dancing 'Waterlilies' with my dear friend Jean Raymond, one of the many partners I had in this short but lovely duet.

When I left Bodenwieser in 1953 I returned to India and Pakistan, then made my way to Europe: (clockwise from top left) a drawing I made later of a dancer in a Delhi palace; dancing at the Metropole Hotel in Karachi; one of my Metropole Hotel wall paintings; life modelling in London; and working on my 'caravan' masks for a performance in London.

Two of my great loves – with Baruch Shadmi in New York (left) and with Bill Tuckwiller in Lewisburg, West Virginia (right). Bill in his usual braces – they were his idea of what a country gentleman should wear.

Right: In Lewisburg I began to dance and choreograph again. This was the mask and costume I made for my dance drama *The Buddha's Wife*.

Below: In New York, Baruch and I spent many years on our aminated film *The Pilgrimage of Truth*, but I also found time for other projects. Here I am painting the story of the 'Song of Songs' on the wall of a Jewish restaurant in Manhattan.

Beth White

A very special birthday – my 108th under the Harbour Bridge, 2022. Always dancing, always surrounded by friends!

Two lovely photos from my recent films with Sue Healey – (top) *Lady of the Horizon*, 2020, and (bottom) *Waterlily Variations*, 2023. I hope life will always keep you – and me – dancing.

It was called *Shikaar*, which I was told meant 'The Hunt'. When my scene was being shot, someone came to fetch me every day in a car. The film studio was a long way from Karachi, in a desert-like area. It was so hot and dry that I had to wrap my head in a damp towel for the journey in order to keep my hair soft and manageable.

The shooting dragged on, and I moved from the Metropole to a smaller family hotel. I had many free days, and to fill the time, I began to develop a new dance drama, based on the story of Princess Siddhartha, wife of the man who would become the Buddha. I had an image of extraordinary creatures – part human, part caravan – a vision of heavy, swaying beasts of burden moving slowly across the Gobi Desert. Their faces came so clearly to me I felt they were begging to be born, and so I began to create strange masks for them out of folded paper. When the masks were made for the princess's caravan they were lined up on the wooden veranda of the hotel where I now lived.

My friends Sigrid and John Kahle invited me to give a show of this work in progress in their home in Karachi. John was cultural attaché for Germany, and he and Sigrid encouraged artists and sometimes produced plays. I had acted in Sigrid's production of the Greek drama *Eurydice*. By now I had a much clearer idea of what would become *The Buddha's Wife*, although I still did not have any expectation of ever seeing it on a stage. I was content at that moment to show the masks and manipulate them myself in a costume of sorts, supposed to represent the caravan leader.

This was my farewell to Karachi. I was now eager to leave for Europe. After packing the masks carefully, I bundled up my clothes and said goodbye to everyone. It was 1957, and I was on my way to London. After three years on my own in India and Pakistan, it felt somehow like I was graduating. Perhaps for the first time, I felt able to take myself seriously as an artist. My India Bag was very full, and the myriad of wondrous experiences I collected have sustained me ever since.

Chapter Nine

Paris / A Frozen Dancer

In London I had a joyful reunion with Evelyn and Bettina, and took a small part in a concert they gave in Australia House, with Marcel as their pianist.

I showed them my 'Caravan' work-in-progress, somewhat more advanced than it had been in Karachi. I also danced Madame's 'Waterlilies' with Bettina, which was always a joyful thing for me to do.

For a few months I stayed with my good friends, the Australian painters, Molly Paxton and Brian Midlane. Brian took a series of photographs of me in dance poses, and I posed for an even larger series of drawings for him in their Pimlico house.

The rest of my time in London was spent enjoying the great museums and art galleries, admiring the Tudor portraits in the National Portrait Gallery, which was directly behind the National Gallery, where I sometimes sat in rapt contemplation of works like the famous *Madonna of the Rocks*.

But now I was anxious to go to Paris, and before six months had passed, I took the train from Waterloo and soon settled into a hotel on Rue Vavin, not far from Gare Montparnasse. The very next day, I was going to visit an old friend – Percival Savage.

❦

On one of our early dance tours in Queensland, we met a young man named Percival Savage. He was backstage to meet the Bodenwieser dancers.

Someone had told Madame he was an artist from a good family who owned a prosperous fruit farm outside of Brisbane. So she approved of him in spite of his tight striped sweater and blue jeans, which contrasted noticeably with the formal attire of other backstage guests.

When Madame had finished introducing him to the group, she turned away and young Percival revealed himself to be a man of great charm and energy.

Somehow, with Percival leading the way, we missed our planned celebratory dinner at an elegant restaurant and ended up in a spaghetti joint he insisted was superb. He was right.

Shortly after that we found ourselves in a taxi because Percival wanted to show us where he had found lodgings after first leaving home – a Chinese temple with all sorts of woodcarvings and artworks he was sure we would love. With no accommodation in sight, he'd been befriended by a Chinese priest, who took him in. After a boisterous night-time expedition, we frightened – and were frightened by – a horse which chased us from the temple grounds.

It was not the end of our evening. Our last stop was the trendy Pink Elephant in yet another part of Brisbane.

As Jean and I settled into our seats we looked up and saw a well-dressed gentleman leading Madame through the doorway. Behind her was a group of people who had been in the green room that evening. She was wearing the black and gold coat I'd made for her and was peering through her lorgnette at the walls around her.

'I see no pink elephant,' she said in her grand lady voice.

She was quite right. There was not a pink elephant in sight – in fact, there were no elephants at all.

At the end of the night, we retired to Percival's house. He showed us his one treasure in the world – a delicate china tea cup he carried with him everywhere.

When our season in Brisbane was over, Percival came to the railway station to see us off. He brought a huge bunch of peacock feathers. Clasping them in his arms, he stood apart from the crowd.

When he saw Madame, he gave them to her.

As the train sped south, away from Brisbane, Madame went to an empty cabin and there she left the peacock feathers. 'They are lovely, but we can't keep them'. She was superstitious, you see, and peacock feathers were known to be unlucky for people in the theatre. We were sorry. Percival had been kind bringing them to us. They were probably dear to him, something he had treasured for their beauty.

None of us expected to see him again. But we were wrong. Three months later he turned up in Sydney, took dancing lessons and got a couple of walk-on parts with the Sydney opera company. About two years later he set out for 'fresh fields and pastures new'. Flying to Adelaide he made his way to the port, where he had organised work as a deckhand on a cargo ship bound for England. That night, there happened to be a violent storm, and the seamen were busy battening things down on deck when Percival went aboard. No one took any notice of him, and he found a sheltered spot and went to sleep. When he woke, the storm was over, and the ship had sailed.

'It was a wonderful night,' Percival told me later. 'Stars like great big diamonds, and a wonderful moon. Only it was the wrong ship!'

By the time the mistake was discovered, it was too late for the ship to turn back. Percival was given a job in the galley assisting the two cooks. There was a fight one night that started because one of the cooks had a rash on his arms and the men objected to him putting his arms into the huge bowl of flour. The cook was killed, the culprit locked up, and Percival given more responsibility.

He pleased the captain because he kept members of the crew busy at night on deck teaching them a dance from *Annie Get Your Gun*. The captain felt this was good for morale and staved off further brawling. But it was really the magical charm of Percival's personality that won the captain over. I was sure of that.

He disembarked in London, but after a day and a half he returned to tell the captain he didn't like London, so they carried him all the way to Marseille. From there he made his way to Paris. He soon made friends and continued to charm people with his infectious giggle, just as he had charmed Madame that night in the green room, and almost everyone he ever met.

ಲ

I had never forgotten Percival, nor the sweet way he had shown off his simple, treasured teacup. When I finally met him again in Paris, he had many, more valuable, treasures in his apartment on the Rue Vaneau, but he looked pleased when I reminded him of the little teacup of his youth. In the time since I'd last seen him, Percival had grown into a man of the world, a celebrated publicity man for Lanvin, a major Paris fashion house. Some things the years hadn't changed – he was still the same eager, generous Percival.

'Look at this.' He opened a trunk and took out a long black gown. 'It's a historical treasure. Try it on if you like but be careful with it.'

It was a creation by the legendary fashion designer, Schiaparelli. If anyone had told me that one day in Paris I would try on a Schiaparelli gown, I don't suppose I would have believed it. Just wearing such a gown made me feel taller, slimmer and more alluring.

I was thinking of André and what he might feel if he saw me at that moment. I was conscious that we were so close, in the same city, and all I had to do if I wanted to see him was look in the telephone book and call him. I wasn't sure I would do that. I didn't know why, but something held me back. It had been over four years since we'd parted. It seemed foolish to me that we had ever gone our separate ways, and I felt that in this Schiaparelli gown I would never do such foolish things. I'd hoped Percival intended on giving it to me, but it was not to be.

He offered a consolation prize: 'If you come to see me at Lanvin tomorrow, we'll dress you like Cinderella.

We'll have dinner at Saint Germain des Prés and afterwards go to a party on the Avenue Foch.'

I did not have to be asked twice. I had come to Paris with the usual lament of all women: 'I have nothing to wear!'

The next day I visited Percival in his office. He looked important sitting behind a desk, answering his house phone and giving orders to someone at the other end of the line, and I was impressed by his self-assured manner. When his tasks were complete, he got up and led me out of the room and along a passage to a large dressing room with two plush couches, lots of mirrors along one wall, gold light fixtures and plush carpet on the floor.

'Wait here.' He went off and came back with a tall, elegant vendeuse in a plain black dress. He and she had a conversation in French, glancing in my direction several times.

'Madame Simone is going to find something for you to wear,' Percival said, then left to attend to more business. I was left with the vendeuse.

Most of my clothes were made of handspun Indian cotton, and I was cold. I had so far purchased only one woollen vest to wear under a sweater. The vendeuse almost fainted with horror when she saw it. 'This! This!' she cried. 'Take it off!'

The offending garment was whisked away and replaced with an elegant black fringed dress. Looking into the wall of mirrors, I saw a whole new Eileen. Or rather, an infinite number of possible Eileens, because of the way I saw myself repeated and reflected in the sections of looking glass.

When Percival came back with a whole bunch of hose of different colours hanging over his arm, he found me looking 'absolutely charming' (so he said) in the fringed dress, as well as an elegant shot-silk taffeta, warmly lined, A-line coat, trimmed with soft bluish-grey mink and a delightful mink hat to match.

'These are from the autumn show. Some of them have never been worn. Look, embroidered beetles on the stockings.' The beetles were tiny ones, just near the ankles.

The vendeuse had forgiven me for the woollen vest. She beamed as Percival led me away to the elevator that carried us to the ground floor. There, I was given expensive makeup and perfume. I went back to Rue Vavin on the Metro carrying this large package with 'Lanvin' printed on it. People looked at me because, in Paris, women who shop in the great fashion houses hardly ever go home on the Metro. I tried not to notice the attention I was attracting.

*

That night we went to a cosy little club frequented by people interested in American jazz music. I did my best to keep up with the Parisian nightlife, and to remain unintimidated by the glamour bombarding me on every side. People were curious about the mysterious Australian woman with the famous publicity man. When they asked, I simply replied, 'Oh, Percival? We're just friends. We're partners. We're a couple of Australian con artists.'

I was trying to be smart like Percival. I could hear him on the other side of the room saying smart things then laughing gaily and heartily, as he always did when he had just said something terribly smart and up-to-the-minute in French.

He didn't laugh at his own cleverness, but at the cleverness of whatever he was talking about. There is a difference.

Then, disaster! Bad for Percival; less so for me. He fractured his ankle and couldn't walk up the three flights to his apartment, so he lent it to me. He went to stay in a hotel almost next door to Lanvin so that he could still go to his work. I was sorry for his calamity, but glad for myself.

Left to my own devices, I toyed with the idea of looking for André in the phonebook but could not bring myself to follow through. Instead, I hid from the winter beneath Percival's electric blanket, and lost myself in elaborate fantasies of running into André by chance. These fantasies could not come true, because I did not go out except to buy ham and olives. I was cold, even in my coat, until I called Percival and he explained how to turn on the heating.

Feeling energetic and grateful, I tidied up. I made order out of chaos. Old newspapers in the bin, postcards gathered up and filed away. Socks were washed and hung up to dry, tiepins and cufflinks polished and secured in a tiny box. I found a place for everything. To help Percival navigate the new order, I made a list of where everything could be found and taped it to the back of the kitchen door.

I was still energetic. With time left over, I began to make a hat out of some leather I found abandoned in a bottom drawer. The leather was covered in strange markings and patterns, and seemed to be crying out to become a garment. I cut and hand-stitched it until it became what I saw in my mind's eye. Pleased with my ingenuity, I donned my new hat and departed for my new accommodation. I felt it was time to move on from Rue Delambre and my dear friend's generosity to a charming hotel I had found near the Sacré Coeur.

*

A few days later, at about nine in the morning, Percival came to my hotel room on his way to work.

'Eileen, thank you for the list on the kitchen door. The only thing I can't find is my Orpheus costume, or part of it. It's a calf skin with symbolic markings on it.'

Percival was very anxious. He was due to visit a costume ball in Belgium and had planned to go as Orpheus. His costume was to be an animal skin – covered in meaningful symbols – to be worn, covering one shoulder, over a Grecian tunic. He told me all about it, until I had to confess: 'Percival, I'm so sorry. I made your costume into a hat.'

I promised to make him another one, with better symbols. I worked in a fever, and soon had a replacement costume – a lyre decal on calfskin, to be worn over a Greek tunic. On his feet would be sandals with silver thongs wound around the lower leg. Percival finished off the outfit with a beautiful headpiece – a garland of green and silver grape leaves on loan from Jean Cocteau. That impressed me terribly.

The costume was complete. There were also two long heavy cloaks made in the Lanvin workroom. These were to save Percival and his companion from freezing to death in Belgium where the ball was to take place. Percival told me afterward that, even with the cloaks, their thongs almost froze onto their bare legs.

While Percival was in Belgium, I made myself at home in my new hotel, and visited his apartment to collect my belongings. On my way out I ran practically headfirst into André, who, as it happened, lived just down the street.

It was like a dream. For the entire month I'd been cloistered at Percival's, dreaming of André, he had been living a few blocks away.

A few minutes later I was walking through the ornate doors to his apartment. Then we were kissing.

'You are living 'ere?! I had no idea. I wanted to send you a message, but I didn't know where to send it.'

I was amazed. It must have been four or five years since we had last seen each other.

Afterwards, it didn't seem as amazing as it did at first. When I looked into his eyes, I could no longer find the man I'd known. The one who'd been infatuated with me, with the idea of timeless love, with Mughal's eternal longing. There were no blissful late afternoons by the emperor's swimming pool. André was no longer the opium-smoking dreamer basking in the great artworks and love stories of a forgotten age. He was now a businessman, with worries and wrinkles, and he had set the dreams of that time aside.

But I was glad to see he still treasured the painting I had given him – the one I had painted of the emperor's girls enjoying themselves in the pool, with the arches in the walls and the wide steps rising on one side to the level of the plain. André took me to a small room and showed it to me, framed and hanging above his desk. We stood and gazed at it sadly, because it was of the past.

I hoped and longed for the past to be repeated, but that is not the way of things. The moments that make up our lives are like those of a dance – no matter how we rehearse, one is never sure if the movement and the music driving us on will align. We soon said goodbye again.

※

Ever since I'd left Madame to see the world, I always thought that I would eventually return to her and rejoin the company. In the years I had been away I'd written regularly to Madame with news of my life – my travels, my romantic ideas and other trivial matters. I asked very little about her. Not once did I inquire about her health. Nor did I make clear how much she meant to me. Then, one day, it was too late.

On 10 November 1959, Madame died of a heart attack in her apartment in Sydney. When news reached me, I was devastated. I have made many mistakes, but I have few regrets. One thing that I do regret deeply is that

I didn't tell Madame Bodenwieser how much she meant to me before she died. I'm sorry that when I was in Paris I didn't write and say, 'Madame, I thank you for all the wonderful joy and beauty and interest and education you brought into my life. You gave me, we, all of us dancers, a beautiful life, and we will always love you for that.'

I missed her. I still miss her very much.

'Madame!' I tell her in my dreams. 'You changed my life. You introduced me to everything that brings me joy!'

But I believe she knew how much she meant to people. Of the effect she had on the lives she touched. She was not ignorant of the gifts she gave us, her dancers. But I would still like to have told her. Or told her I was sorry if I had ever contradicted her or spoken tactlessly, as I know I sometimes had.

Back in Australia, the rest of the dancers were just as distraught. I think most of us thought that Madame would always be in our lives. We knew that she had come to Australia because of a most terrible fate, but from that darkness she brought something truly wonderful to all our lives, and to Australia too. Australia needed Madame Bodenwieser, just as we girls did, and now she was gone.

When Emmy had recovered from her grief – which was intense, for she had always been very close to Madame –

she and Marie Cuckson, one of Madame's students, gathered all the photographs and papers they could find about Madame's dances. After much painstaking work – which was continued tirelessly by Marie's daughter, Barbara – Madame's archives were donated to the National Library of Australia in Canberra.

I learned that Margaret (Chappie) Chapple had taken over the direction of the school, and that Coralie Hinkley, who had always loved Madame, had returned from four years study of modern dance in America, and was now a senior dance teacher in one of Sydney's leading schools. The group had broken up, and although Chappie continued to teach the Central European expressive style she'd learned from Madame, she included other styles of dance beyond the strict school of Bodenwieser.

I could not see a place for me as a dancer back in Sydney. I had always meant to return to Madame and had never envisioned a future without her. Now, I would have to find another.

Chapter Ten

New York / Stop Motion

After Madame's death and my disappointment over André, I shunned cafe society and other members of the human race, preferring to keep to myself. I made no attempt to dance but found a place for myself in the art world as an artist's model.

Each studio had its own professor teaching his own style of painting – abstract or figurative. The battle lines seemed fiercely drawn in Paris, but I stayed neutral, kept my eyes and ears open, and in a way received free tuition while at the same time earning enough each week to pay my hotel bill and other expenses. I had enough to live comfortably, although not in luxury.

I was not at all unhappy modelling instead of dancing. I liked the stillness of modelling, and I liked the drawing classes where I gave one-minute poses, which I still thought of as 'frozen dances'. Those sessions were good for me, in that they gave me a sense of performing for an audience. The rest of the time, I preferred solitude.

Alone in my attic at night, I liked to look out my window at the rooftops of Montparnasse. It made me think of the stories in books I had read when I lived on Phillip Street. How far I had come, in some ways, only to start again.

I began to write. I had moonlighted as a correspondent for magazines in Australia – publishing stories and observations from my travels in India. *The Women's Weekly* was particularly interested in stories of exotic places and people, and so I began to write dispatches about living alone in Paris – the food, the culture, the cutthroat game of trying to find a hotel at a decent price that never seemed to end. The editors at *The Women's Weekly* were very good to me, and published whatever story I sent. Their enthusiasm energised me.

I began to write a science-fiction novel about a group of time travellers called 'Helionians'. They came from a distant future when Earth was called 'Heliotrope'. Montparnasse, with its cafes and its Rue de la Grande Chaumière, was one of the locations from which much of the story evolved. Almost everyone I had met since coming to Paris, and others who came from somewhere else, crowded its pages. Some, like Percival, were easily recognisable, but they all had new names. Picasso appeared as Mario, one of the time travellers. He created futuristic paintings made of light in the sky over Paris that amazed everyone. A rogue's gallery of remarkable people and their time-lapse adventures became my companions in the attic in the Rue de la Gaité as I burned the midnight oil writing my book.

One evening in 1962, without realising it, I must have felt the need of other company. After dining alone at a noisy, cheerful student restaurant for artists and intellectuals called Le Foyer des Artistes (these days, like all great bohemian institutions, it has become a bank), I walked back along Boulevard du Montparnasse. Le Select, a brasserie on the corner of Rue Vavin, was buzzing. It was usually so crowded that I tended to avoid it, but this time I stepped onto its terrace and seated myself at the only empty table. The waiter soon came, and I ordered a demitasse.

The group of people at the next table was talking loudly, all at once, about film. I couldn't help hearing some of the conversation, in particular one man, who was speaking more loudly and passionately than all the rest.

The group grew larger, and rowdier, and soon overflowed to my table. I welcomed them.

Suddenly, I found that the loud, intense man who'd talked about film was sitting beside me, talking to me as if he'd known me for a long time.

After a while, I told him about my experiences of movie-making when the Bodenwieser company had performed in *Spotlight on Australian Ballet*, and when I had danced in the Pakistani film.

I didn't expect he would be impressed, yet he took what I said quite seriously.

His name was Baruch Shadmi – a Polish émigré who now lived in New York and made films. He looked like a filmmaker – with rich dark hair groomed into orderly waves, and deep grey eyes that sparkled with joy and excitement when he talked about art.

He told me he was trying to form a company to make art documentaries, including ones about dance. He had recently made a successful dance film with music by Leonard Bernstein in New York.

Before I left the cafe to return to my attic that night, I had promised to have dinner with him the following evening. We dined together that night and for the next four nights.

On the fourth night, he told me he had to leave Paris the next day but expected to return in three months' time.

He asked me to wait for him, 'Then I want you to be mine forever.' I was surprised and could not quite believe it.

⁂

While Baruch was away we exchanged letters, and in exactly three months he came back as he said he would. After a few weeks he asked me to move into his hotel with him. Although I did so, I didn't quite understand my feelings for him, nor his for me. It was clear that we had a strong connection, although it felt like no love affair I'd ever had before. It was like an ocean journey – sometimes calm, often stormy.

While I lived in Paris, Jean Raymond and I corresponded regularly. Jean was in New York, staying with Maryat Lee, a playwright she had met in Hong Kong. Maryat had made a name for herself with her play *Dope*. It was a street theatre drama about the problems of drug trafficking on the Upper East Side and had caused quite a stir for graphic scenes.

After the success of *Dope*, Maryat continued working with the group of untrained actors she had formed in Harlem, while at the same time producing another of her plays, *The Tightrope Walker*, with professional actors in an off-Broadway theatre.

I had the impression from Jean's letters that life in Greenwich Village with Maryat Lee was full of interest and excitement. Maryat had the gift of discovering and bringing out talents in other people. Under her influence, Jean had – in addition to the Martha Graham dance classes – enrolled in one of the foremost drama schools in New York, where the Stanislavski method was taught. Maryat had also encouraged Jean to write, and as I was Jean's closest friend, she also took an interest in my writing and in me.

This encouraged me to send them a story I had written after a recent train journey from Paris to Athens. It featured a remarkable vision I'd had, in which my consciousness took leave from my body, and zoomed along the length of the train, with a view of all the strange and unusual things happening onboard.

Jean and Maryat read my story and Jean had a go at editing it. Something must have happened to her at the Stanislavski drama school as she cut out all the parts about my flying along beside the train. Without that, I considered it a rather dull story. This depressed me somewhat. But a few days later another letter came from Jean in which she apologised – Maryat had read the edited version of my story and told her to put it all back as it was. Every word.

I showed my story and Jean's letter to Baruch. He agreed with Maryat, nodding seriously. He respected all creative efforts: writing, painting, acting, dancing – even more, perhaps, than I did. I knew that I craved approval and delighted in praise – my works were love offerings, for which I hoped to have my love returned. Yet the work itself was of great interest to me too. I was always trying to learn and hoped that I might one day rise above my longing for approval.

As for Baruch's project, it did not seem to be progressing. He had several meetings with his prospective partners and even signed a contract of sorts. He showed me a photograph taken of the signing – Baruch seated at a large desk, hand poised above the sheet of paper, smile wide and confident. Around the table, a group of well-dressed men witnessing the signing gave me a sense of unreality.

'Why don't you go back to New York and make your own documentary? On your own terms? Another film about dance or some painter whose work inspires you?' I wanted to say.

But Baruch didn't want to do it that way. He wanted a company with big offices, employees running in and out, telephones ringing and secretaries to answer them. Just as strong as his passion for the arts was Baruch's craving for success. He had always been eager for it. Perhaps too eager.

Baruch became so impatient with how slowly the project progressed that he threatened to sue. Somehow his partners slipped out of the contract and at last Baruch agreed that we should move to New York.

Maryat had invited me to stay in her New York apartment for the summer. We planned that I would travel ahead and wait for Baruch while he wrapped up loose ends in Paris.

I chose to go by sea, and before I left, Baruch and I decided to spend three weeks in Dieppe, on the north coast of France. What we had together was more like a honeymoon than a farewell.

The only attraction in the town, apart from a lonely windswept beach still littered with pillboxes from the allied landing on D-Day, was the casino.

Late each afternoon we went there. It had marble terraces, gardens, balconies, long halls, rooms, a bar and restaurant, and the gaming room. To gain admittance to the wide room with the gaming tables, you had to sit in a small antechamber and pose while an artist made a crayon sketch of your face. It was a tradition left over from before the days of cameras, but one that Baruch liked. He had already posed for his likeness, and it was filed away. Mine was not because the artist wasn't at his post the afternoon we tried to visit. So Baruch went in to play and I wandered off along the hallway towards the terrace.

On the way, I was distracted by the sounds of jazz music. I stepped through a doorway and entered a large ballroom, splendidly furnished with crimson velvet couches, curtains, sparkling chandeliers and a beautifully polished dance floor. I knew very little about the jazz musicians of America, but I'd seen Ella Fitzgerald play in Paris, and I recognised the leader of this band because of the funny way his face screwed up when he smiled. He smiled now and gestured for me to enter the otherwise empty hall.

For the next twenty minutes I had a singular encounter with Louis Armstrong and his group. They played for me, and I danced for them. I had them all to myself, and they taught me to dance 'The Twist'. The bass player, a giant man, ran his fingers suggestively up and down the strings while grinning wickedly at me, but it was only in fun.

As soon as they stopped playing to take their rest, I left the ballroom, wandering back along the hallway and out onto the white stone terrace where the night air from the English Channel cooled me.

At the end of our three-week holiday, Baruch took me to Cherbourg where I was to board the *Queen Elizabeth II* for New York. He saw me off from the wharf, promising to follow me as soon as he could. I leaned over the ship's railing and waved goodbye.

After an uneventful voyage across the Atlantic, I was surprised to find Maryat waiting for me when the ship docked in Manhattan. Somehow, in all the chaos of the New York docks, she had found me! I felt flattered and safe as she helped me with my luggage. Passing through immigration was not difficult as I had my visa and passport and her reassuring presence. There was an air of authority about her that commanded respect.

When we reached her 6th Avenue apartment, Maryat was hospitable, and showed me to a room I felt instantly at home in. We went out for dinner to an Italian restaurant on Bleecker Street, and I realised I was in an area known as Little Italy that Baruch had spoken about with fondness over many meals.

Weeks passed and Baruch did not come. Nor did he write many letters. I began to doubt him. I wasn't exactly lonely but the social scene in New York wasn't the buzzing, bohemian hive I'd expected. I didn't meet any of the artists or actors Jean had written about in her letters.

Maryat herself would spend the summer in her house at the edge of a lake in New Jersey, so I had the apartment to myself. Unlike many New Yorkers who let their apartments when they went away for the summer, she did not ask me to pay any rent. She asked only that I write twenty pages of new writing each week and send them to her. She would then write her comments in the margins and send them back to me.

Doing so seemed to be an impossible task, but Maryat had a way of inspiring the impossible. Every Friday I walked up to the Greenwich Village post office and mailed a fat envelope with twenty pages in it. Sometimes I wrote my thoughts, sometimes pages of dialogue, and sometimes I found myself writing stories. I wrote several stories: some of them not bad. I felt sometimes as if I was pulling a long string of words and sentences out of my head as a silkworm pulls the silken thread out of its body.

By the time I would be ready to make the next trip to the post office, the previous week's pages were returned with her comments. I read them eagerly. Her words were precious to me, even if they were sometimes critical. On occasion, she showed my writing to other writers she was acquainted with.

Maryat was Southern royalty, in a sense, because she was a descendent of Robert E. Lee, the Civil War general who remains a folk hero in the South. This meant she was well acquainted with all sorts of interesting people from that part of the world, including the great Southern Gothic writer Flannery O'Connor. Maryat was kind enough to send her one of my stories about a boat journey to get her opinion and she was kind enough to write back. Kind in her uniquely direct Southern Gothic way:

Dear Eileen:

I like your story fine and I would not advise you to do anything to it but type it plain and spell it right and send it to some of the smaller literary magazines. Get Maryat to spellit [sic] to you if the dear girl can spell any better than you can, which I doubt. Failing her, get the dictionary. You write like a painter, very solid. I like it because I can see it, because it is all clear. I think you can really write about things. I don't know yet if you can write about people: but what you have done here in this story with things seen is wonderful.

I hope you found your boat and your cabin in it and that you did not slip through the floor and spend the night in the innards of the engine. If you did I am sure you saw some interesting sights.

Best Regards,
Signed.
F. O'Connor

The only other contact I had with people was when I went to the enormous supermarket once a week. I enjoyed the air-conditioning, for the streets of Manhattan were stifling that summer. I also enjoyed the music that made it pleasant to push the shopping basket dreamily along the aisles. In Paris I had not shopped very much for food, but when I did, I went to the street markets. Supermarket shopping was a new experience. Who could have imagined the abundance that Americans lived with? I'd never owned a refrigerator in my life, and it was somewhat surreal to walk through rows and rows of frozen meals.

I was curious about Baruch's whereabouts, as he had still not materialised. I received a letter from Belgium. What could he be doing there? His letter told me nothing about his business. They were supposed to be love letters, yet I found them puzzling. Although he spoke English very well, he wrote some very funny things.

For instance, he described the scene when my ship left Cherbourg. In his recollection, he looked up and saw my 'watery blue eyes as you wept at our parting'. I had no recollection of weeping, and besides, my eyes are not blue, but a shade of hazel.

It was six months before Baruch finally reached New York. He came to Maryat's apartment, but she was suspicious of him and told me he could not stay there. He then surprised her by immediately going uptown on the day of his arrival and coming back two hours later to say he had taken an apartment for us. The next day I said goodbye to Maryat and dutifully followed Baruch to the place he had found on East 91st Street.

We were happy in our new home, a five-room furnished apartment in a building that may once have been a hotel. The rooms were spacious with lofty ceilings. They were already furnished after a fashion, but we changed curtains, bed covers, and hung pictures on the walls. To make it homier, we scavenged a desk, a bookcase and a new chair from the street. I learned quickly that scavenging for discarded furniture in New York was no joke. People took it very seriously – and I was so impressed I wrote a story about it for an Australian magazine. So, we had furniture. Still no refrigerator.

The living room, further back, had a door opening onto the landing and staircase. The kitchen had no door, only a window opening to a fire escape overlooking 92nd Street at the rear of the building. When I was alone in the apartment that fire escape made me nervous. It looked as if anyone could climb up from the street and come in through the window, but no one ever did.

I often gazed out at sunset and watched a group of men squatting on the pavement of East 92nd Street rolling dice. In the light of the setting sun they looked exactly as if Rembrandt had painted them.

Our apartment came with a vast basement where Baruch stored his movie-making equipment. It waited down there for him, while he waited for inspiration. In the meantime, several homeless cats moved in, preferring the sooty, gloomy basement to the freezing streets of New York.

One day, as I visited the basement to fetch something from a trunk, I heard tiny little footsteps, and from the darkness, meowing pitifully but looking wonderfully pretty, came a tiny little grey and white cat with deep blue eyes.

When I picked her up, she wriggled and jumped and scampered off into the darkness again. I fed her every day and, after exactly a week, as though I'd passed a rehearsal, she trotted after me and begged to be taken upstairs.

We named her Pusilla, and she made herself at home. She was the sweetest little cat you could imagine, although her time in the basement had given her an anxiety complex about food. If left alone with her dinner, she would eat so much she would swell up for two days.

So, trips to the basement proved fruitful. Soon enough, Baruch went back down for his film gear and recovered from his failure to form a company abroad. He was too driven and too full of ideas to hold still for long.

One day Baruch saw me crafting. I'd been sitting about and happened to have some fine white paper and a jar of Elmer's glue. My hands began their work, and soon I'd made a small, white figurine. It was the figure of Truth, from Madame's dance drama, 'The Pilgrimage of Truth'. Madame's drama was adapted from a medieval folk tale that became a morality play. In the 1920s it was staged on a more elaborate scale in Germany. Madame Bodenwieser, who had worked as choreographer for the great director Max Reinhardt, choreographed it as one of her first dance dramas, and repeated it when she came to Australia, where I'd inherited one of the roles.

Now that I found myself crafting the lead character, I was not sure what I would do with it. To be honest, I was not sure why I had created it, until Baruch looked over my shoulder and asked what I was making.

I told him that it was Truth, and explained the story behind Madame's drama, and he surprised me by saying: 'We could make an animated film of that story.'

I was taken with the idea and immediately set to work to create the other characters in Truth's journey. Baruch soon gave himself over completely to his new project. It was not going to be a big money maker, but I expected it to be good for the soul. To work on something small and true was what I'd wanted him to do since he'd first become entangled with those pompous film producers in Paris.

I would have been content to make a ten- or fifteen-minute film, but Baruch had grander visions. For the next few years, until 1966, we gave it all our attention and creative energy. Since Baruch did not bother me with details about his financial affairs, I didn't even think about the cost. I had no idea where the money for our project came from. I made all the figures myself, and we brought them to life in various ways – physically moving them around on wires or sticks, or using stop-motion – shooting a few frames, moving the figures and shooting again. Our sets were dioramas, which Pusilla would enjoy exploring. Occasionally she found her way into a shot, making her own 'artistic contribution'.

To supplement the animation, we filmed stretches of live action in which I played Truth come to life, dancing in all sorts of locations from Central Park to a surreal folly of a house crafted from a mountain of junk.

Baruch taught me to edit film, a practice that at once demands the most precise accuracy, and a blind leap of faith, trusting one's instincts. I was amazed at how cutting a single frame could change the entire meaning of the thing. It was a long, long process.

Editing *The Pilgrimage of Truth* made me think back to the 1948 documentary about Australian ballet that had featured several Bodenwieser dances. Much of the footage of me seemed to have ended up on the cutting room floor. The director, Doc Sternberg, had included a sequence of Ann Pitsch and me performing 'Waterlilies' outdoors, rising up in our delicate waterlily costumes beside a lily pond. Apparently, I was also seen in a close up somewhere in 'The Blue Danube', and briefly as a spinning cog in 'The Demon Machine'. But that was it. At the time it bothered me, but as I learned to edit, I grew more forgiving. The truth is, a strip of six or ten frames between the thumb and finger in the editing room feels sizeable enough, but you had better not blink when you're sitting in the screening room looking at the film.

Looking back at yourself in moving pictures is not the same as looking at photographs. To see yourself alive, moving with your hair dancing around your cheeks, eyes larger, your waist and hips smaller, is a moving experience.

Because time has passed and you were younger, you feel free to express tenderness for that person who is yourself yet is another person whom you have not seen for a long time – and, had you only known it, you have missed. You feel no guilt for your conceit when you look twice to enjoy your own prettiness and to see how young and tender you were.

The film Baruch and I were making was a vast labour of love. We worked hard – painstakingly cutting, joining, discarding, recutting. Pusilla pounced joyfully on the fragments that found their way to the cutting room floor, skittering through the apartment as the film slipped beneath her paws.

༄

We were only halfway through the editing process when Baruch suffered a stroke. He spent six months in the hospital, but he worked very diligently, exercising and doing whatever the physical therapist advised. I visited him, and filmed his recovery to make a fifteen-minute film, ending with his first walk out onto the street. Soon, we were able to resume work on *The Pilgrimage of Truth*, but by then, all Baruch's money had been used up in payment for the hospital bills.

Baruch, undaunted, applied for funds to finish the film. He was awarded enough to pay for the mixing of the soundtrack and the final printing.

A truckload of ten 35-millimeter film cans containing the finished product was delivered to us, and in November of 1967 we gave a private screening to friends and people in the moving picture business. Watching the final version was strangely surreal. It ended up running one hundred and twenty minutes. At the time, I believe it may have been the longest animated film in the world.

We then showed our film down on Canal Street, where alongside the other filmmakers showing their abstract, often sex-mad pictures, our graceful morality tale drew polite applause and praise. I'm not sure the other, avant-garde filmmakers really appreciated our film. At the time, the gratuitous, the edgy, and the ugly were all in vogue, and none of that was to my taste, so I didn't really mind. Baruch and I loved the film, especially the shot near the end, where Pusilla's tail could clearly be seen crossing a castle drawbridge.

༺༻

Baruch never fully recovered from his stroke. By the end of 1968, I had become his helper. I had agreed to be responsible for looking after him following his discharge from hospital, and was now, effectively, his nurse. In some ways, I felt enslaved by him. I no longer thought of myself as a dancer. My life was completely bound to his.

It was true that Baruch behaved unreasonably. His strong emotions, once channelled into passion and love of art, were now coming out in other ways. He would sit in his chair, frustrated that he could not stand,

and would start to grow angry. The only thing that soothed him then would be Pusilla, who would cross the floor, sit in front of him, and blink slowly at him. He would calm down immediately.

The social worker and doctors at the hospital were aware of our struggles. They believed Baruch was demanding more of me than was good for either of us, so they suggested a change in our domestic arrangement. They said I should find somewhere else to stay and organise a home attendant, not related personally to him, to visit him on weekdays, while I should stay with him on the weekends.

I took their advice and went to stay with a friend on West 57th Street. The new arrangement was better for me. Baruch didn't like it, but in his more reasonable moments he accepted it. He even said once that I should leave him so he could get better on his own.

During this time he grew weaker and had to undergo heart surgery. He slowly recovered only to return to the hospital a few years later with another serious complaint from which he did not recover. He died in the hospital one cold night in April 1987.

I realised that I'd known Baruch, his hopes and desires and his passion for life, the good and the bad, and his realities and his unrealities, his self-destructive power, and his creative power, but I had never really known whether our love was real.

There were so many complexities and contradictions in our relationship that I was often in doubt. I'd always had to submit to his will and do his bidding. Naturally I discussed this question of what was love and what was enslavement with Maryat who, as an advocate of women's liberation, said Baruch was a male chauvinist and I was a co-dependent. That may have been true, but we had been happy in our creative life together. Was this what Baruch had recognised in me when he asked me to be his forever – something deeper between us than romantic love?

*

After Baruch's death I was left with a sense of freedom, but I was also left with grief. It was not for my own loss but for his. I had shared so many emotions with him and had seen his dreams come to nothing. In his death I inherited the echo of his rage and his frustration. Yet I had learned much from him. I cried for him every night before I fell asleep and thought of him as a tragic hero who had strived so hard to attain his ideal that he never found satisfaction in life.

Before he died, Baruch sold all his film equipment and gave the money to me. It was all he had left.

With this, I went back to France and stayed with a friend in Normandy.

Of all the places I had lived or visited, France held a special place in my heart. And a memory came to me, from the time I had been working as an artist's model in Paris, before I had met Baruch. It was the story of an encounter with an earthworm, a small creature, just a scrap of life. But it had shown me something about myself then and it could do so again.

I had made a trip south to the Cote d'Azur with my friend, Jane, an English girl I had met in the art schools, who had a car. After driving for miles on a long, hot road we came across a small general store which looked, to these thirsty travellers, like a spot we might buy some lemonade. Jane parked in the shade of a tree opposite the store, and in I went.

Bonjour, merci, to the shopkeeper, and I left with a precious bottle of French lemonade. The cold drink was very welcome; it was ferociously hot, even for the French summer. The black road stretched off into the distance, shimmering with the day's heat.

I took a moment to contemplate. The day, the cold drink in my hand, the hot road beneath my feet. As I was about to return to the car, I looked down and saw something that made me pause. It was an earthworm, long and pink, apparently beginning the long journey across the road.

I bent over to watch it more closely and found myself intrigued by its movements. First it would extend the front part of its body, which got thinner as a result. Then it would draw forward its middle section, bunched and rounded, to fill out its front thin section, while the last section moved up to become fat and rounded in turn. The front then got long and thin again, and the middle and rear parts repeated their movements.

The worm went through this sequence, again and again, making its way in the world. I watched, fascinated, in a kind of scientific exultation. This humble creature was a miracle of movement.

My sense of wonder gave way to alarm when I realised that the poor creature had a vast journey in front of it, across the scorching bitumen. I ran to some bushes growing on the roadside, chose the softest leaf I could find and set it down as a little carriage for the worm.

It took advantage, got busy with its clever front-middle-rear sequence, and slid aboard. I picked up the leaf and carried the worm to safety, where it disappeared into the earth to continue its day's work.

Back in the car, as we opened our bottle of lemonade, Jane asked me what I'd been doing, 'bending over the road like that.'

'I was saving the life of an earthworm,' I replied.

'Oh,' said Jane without blinking, 'alright. Let's go.'

She started the car and on we went towards the Cote d'Azur.

Exactly what it was about that encounter that so touched me, and made me remember it so clearly, I'm not sure. At the time, I think it reminded me that whatever else I was – artist's model, painter, writer – I was, in essence, a dancer, that movement was at the heart of it all.

This realisation still held true, but there was also something in the memory that made me think about acceptance. Perhaps, like my little friend the worm, I needed to accept an unusual turn of circumstance and just keep wriggling along, towards whatever destination lay ahead.

Six months passed in Normandy and in Paris before I decided to go back to New York. There, I bought a train ticket, gave up the apartment Baruch and I had lived in, and went to the town of Lewisburg, West Virginia, where Maryat Lee had been living for the last year. I needed to reconnect with myself as an artist.

Chapter Eleven

West Virginia / Just You Wait

In the summer of 1988, the train from New York pulled into the White Sulphur Springs station, where Maryat was waiting for me. She had given up her house in Powley's Creek – the 'Women's Farm', where she had been running summer theatre programs for young people – and moved to the nearby town of Lewisburg.

The drive to her home took less than fifteen minutes, and we pulled up outside a large Southern-style house with dormer windows and white columns propping up a long white porch.

It was at the end of the street, next to a long field of rolling hills. In the fading evening light, the hills looked like an impressionist painting, with the endless mountains of West Virginia rising behind them like cut-outs of fine purple-grey chiffon, layered one against the other, fading away until the most distant curved mountaintop appeared to dissolve into a light finer than mist.

Because Maryat was a descendant of Robert E. Lee, she had what the West Virginians call 'clout'. We ate a salad that her friend had prepared for us, then Maryat showed me where she now produced her plays – two rooms made into one at the front of the house, with a platform built at one end as a theatre.

The lovely bedroom she had set aside for me was also at the front, and such was Maryat's generous nature, it was larger than her own room, which was tucked away at the back of the house. My room had something I'd always wanted – a deep bay window. It also had a four-poster bed with a fringed canopy. The only other articles of furniture were an old-fashioned wardrobe, a comfortable chair and a dressing table with three silver-framed photographs of Maryat: as a child of four, a child of ten and a serious young college girl. She had been beautiful then, and she still was, with her very attractive smile and the soft charm of her Southern accent. But in choosing to make herself look strong, it was as if she had decided to give up on beauty. Her clothes were as plain as she could make them. Part of me was disappointed by this, as I had made her a very romantic dress that suited her very well when I had first known her in New

York. But I could see I had to abandon those visions and accept her as she was now.

Another change I began to notice was in her theatre work. Rather than staging her own plays, Maryat was now more interested in the stories that might emerge from within a group of untrained actors. She gathered young people together and taught them to write and direct their own plays as well as act in them. These plays were genuine and heartfelt. There was one about a house that felt lonely because no one lived in it, and another about waiting for a cousin to come back from Vietnam. It wasn't just about the plays though. She still had her magical way of drawing out the creative spirit in people, as she had done for me in New York. She had something of a sixth sense for untapped potential.

A bit later I ran into a young woman who I knew had been part of one of Maryat's theatre groups; she was working as a cashier in a supermarket in Lewisburg. This woman had been so terribly shy she could hardly speak or meet anyone's eye. I asked her whether working under Maryat had helped her; she just smiled the most radiant smile: 'Yes.'

❦

Maryat's gift for connection also extended to matters of the heart. I had been in Lewisburg for about three weeks when she told me she was planning a small party for me. She wanted to introduce me to a widower.

'Oh, Maryat. I don't want to meet any fat, old, bald bank managers,' I told my friend. Then, realising I was being rather rude, I apologised.

Maryat only laughed and assured me that this gentleman wasn't any of those things. His name was William 'Bill' Tuckwiller, and he was a seventh generation West Virginian. He had about forty-five cousins in the Greenbrier Valley. In these parts, where you could live for fifty years and still be considered a stranger, these were highly sought-after qualities, but in truth, I wasn't very interested.

I had no desire to meet any kind of man so soon after Baruch's death. I had stopped crying at night, to be sure. In a way his passing had released me, yet I still thought about him and his life with sadness in my heart. I wasn't going to forget him. I wouldn't forget anyone. The men I had loved had enriched my life. Each one had touched me deeply, but Baruch had taken charge of my life, and in many ways, I had forgotten myself.

So, during the course of the party, I paid little attention to Bill – although I did note that he was not the frumpy old widower I'd imagined. On the contrary, he was slim, tall enough, with thick hair and a self-assured, courteous and cool demeanour.

I must have made some kind of impression because after the party he dawdled on the porch, watching the night sky for bats, and when we joined him, he asked us, 'Would you ladies join me for dinner?'

We went as three to the Chinese restaurant in town, where I left most of the conversation to Maryat and Bill. He regaled us with stories of sailing with his late wife in Caribbean waters, and of serving in the navy in the war. I tried to picture this man handling a boat the way my father had and found I could not. He seemed too gentle to be wrestling with the waves.

Soon afterwards, I ran into Bill in town, where he invited me to go for a drive in his Bronco. We drove for some time through the most beautiful countryside, and every so often Bill would point out some detail – a shining duck pond, the halo of light at the peak of a mountain. I enjoyed letting myself be carried into the unknown. Yet I could not help wondering whether I was on a date, or whether he looked upon me as a tourist who needed to be shown the sights.

After a long drive, we parked and walked along a path that ran beside a stream that ended in a waterfall, which in turn filled a pond. Nearby was a charming little restaurant. I have always loved romantic country spots such as this, so I was feeling very pleased with Bill for taking me there. After so many years of paying hospital bills and forgoing simple pleasures, I had almost forgotten how it felt to walk into a restaurant like this with a man.

We were given a table on a candle-lit veranda overlooking the waterfall.

The only other diners were seated at the far end, and we could hear only the murmur of their voices as they spoke softly, and the clinking of their glasses as they appeared to be toasting each other. I began to remember other such restaurants, on warm nights such as this, in other countries. Even though this was an entirely new experience for me, it felt very comfortable and warm already.

It wasn't until the dessert was served that we really looked into each other's eyes. We were suddenly united in our greedy delight. The dessert was a key lime pie with the crispiest crust and masses of whipped cream slowly sliding down and dripping over the sides.

'This is like heaven!' I told him. He agreed. The moment came to an end, but this marked the beginning of our courtship.

Courtship was the word for it – Bill was the epitome of a Southern gentleman, and did not rush the romance. He got to know me very slowly, while just as gradually revealing the many charms of West Virginia. In all honesty, he could have been less gentlemanly; I wouldn't have minded. On one of our first dates, we went to pick blueberries; it seemed very important to him, so I dug deep into myself and found some enthusiasm for blueberries. Another time he took me to the top of a nearby mountain and showed me the ruins of a summerhouse that had been struck by lightning and burned down. All that remained was an old claw-footed bathtub with wild roses peeping over the edge like maidens having a bath together. It was there that I 'accidentally' tripped and fell into his arms.

Bill and I fell in love, in a very slow, romantic way. Sometimes I saw in him a Buddha-like quality. He was a quiet, calm observer of the world. He appreciated nature, and the natural way of things, and took life as it came, showing very little interest in railing against the world.

He seemed to be content at heart – free of tormenting thoughts. I'm not sure how true these ideas were that I had about him. I could have been wrong, but my growing impression was of an uncomplicated but fundamentally kind man.

Our drives continued. I thought he might like music. As my contribution to our outings, I took some CDs for our entertainment. We would cruise through valleys, up mountains and down again listening to song after song. We were from very different worlds, but in between Patsy Cline and Edith Piaf, we found some common ground.

One evening, as we were sitting in Bill's television room watching a film about American jazz, Bill suddenly began to feel breathless. He asked me to call an ambulance, which I did, but his condition worsened and I was afraid he would not reach the hospital alive. Poor Bill was quite blue by the time he was installed in the emergency ward.

I had called Bill's daughter Lucie, who in turn called the minister of their church. Lucie went in to see Bill first and took the churchman with her. The minister asked if Bill would like to say a prayer.

'I don't reckon so,' said Bill. He'd stopped going to church years earlier.

By the time I was finally allowed in to see him and stand by the bed, he had his colour back and could breathe a little easier.

His other daughter, Sue, made arrangements for him to be moved to another hospital, where her husband practiced medicine. Tests were run, and a heart condition was diagnosed. With Lucie, Sue and I at his bedside, Bill put on a brave face.

'How long have I got?' he asked the doctor.

The doctor looked grave, as he chose his words. 'Two years.'

We were utterly shocked. I had expected the doctor to say, 'You're perfectly all right. You can go home now.'

We did go home. We went home together. I moved in with Bill, into his house on Jefferson Street with a big back garden. We would, as it turned out, have nine happy years together; many more than the doctor's prediction.

Bill's place was a grand old Antebellum home – like something out of *Gone with the Wind*. Enormous, gold-leaf mirrors hung on the walls, and antique Chinese carpets ran underfoot. Those carpets were so lovely I was scared to walk on them lest I leave behind my footprints.

The furniture was handmade, and handpicked by the first Mrs Tuckwiller, who had built a delightful home for her and Bill. I was in awe of it, and happy to find myself living my life as Ms Eileen Tuckwiller (although we never married). All of a sudden, for the first time in my life, I owned a refrigerator, and it was full of American food.

Sometimes we ate at home and sometimes we went to local restaurants like the Eagle's Nest or to Granny's Kitchen for fried eggs and bacon and grits, and to the warm spring baths nearby. Quite often I cooked at home and Lucie and her husband Ron came for dinner.

We rescued an abandoned cat and dubbed him Mr Puss. The cat had once had another name, but I took to calling him Mr Puss. After a while, I'd been calling him Mr Puss for so long, I thought it was about time I officially changed his name.

Mr Puss, like me, found himself unexpectedly happy so late in life. We loved that cat, and that cat appreciated us. He would join us for mealtimes and sit patiently, like a proper Southern gentleman, waiting for titbits from the table to be served up. He had a velvet cushion he liked to sit on. We were all so comfortable.

'I feel like Bill, this life, is my reward,' I once told Maryat over tea, 'for having looked after Baruch all those years.'

Baruch had been a wild man who liked trouble, and courted angst and misery. In many ways, Bill was his opposite. Although we met many years after we came into the world, Bill was truly the love of my life.

When a young person asks me about love, or worries that they have never really fallen in love, I tell them, 'Just you wait. Just. You. Wait. It's on its way.'

It doesn't matter if you haven't found your great love yet. Because I found the best love of my life at a time when I thought there would be no more new love. There was no limit to it. Before Bill, I always fell in love with the wrong man. Which has its place in a lifetime, yes, but it's nice to finally find the real thing.

As well as falling in love, I had also gradually been finding my feet again as an artist in Lewisburg.

In 1989, before I moved in with Bill, I had taken over an apartment from one of Maryat's friends in an old bank building that had been repurposed for a small colony of creative people. The building was a centre for students, artists, dancers and craftspeople, which would eventually become the Trillium Performing Arts Collective, named for a lovely white flower that grows wild in West Virginia.

In every room some kind of creative project was in progress. My next-door neighbour was a weaver with an enormous loom, and she inspired me to create my own textile artwork – a giant wall hanging with layers of fabric representing the vast West Virginia mountains, and a tiny figure with a fishing rod in the foreground. This was, in a way, a tribute to Bill.

Elsewhere, people explored all sorts of artistic pursuits: mime, piano lessons, theatre – and dance.

When I first moved in, I had noticed a dance school upstairs called The Dance Studio. As well as running children's classes, the group of dancers who taught there also put on a concert each year for the joy of it. I was attracted by the studio, but afraid to set foot in it. During my long period as Baruch's nurse, I had not danced, except for what I had done in our film. Otherwise, it had been twenty years since I'd really danced.

One morning I couldn't resist anymore. I joined an improvisation class, and it was as though part of me came back to life.

The improv class was run by a dancer called Beth White. I found her ideas intriguing. One exercise involved all of us standing together, whispering to each other, hissing. The resulting sound gave me a vivid idea for a new and exciting dance work. The following week I suggested to Beth that we have a recording made of the whispers. With the earnestness that improv students are capable of, the group whispered until our throats protested, and the recording was made.

I took this to a composer within Trillium, Robert Wilson, and asked him to write a score for the dance work I had in mind – one that began with a cacophony of whispers.

It didn't take very long for him to give me a recording of the whole score. With this I was able to start rehearsals.

The images were so clear to me, and with the perfect cast I had managed to assemble, the thirty-minute dance work was formed quickly, all perfectly clear and bright. It was called 'Whispers, Cries and Angels'. It had something of Bodenwieser in it, but it was quite different.

In 1992 we gave a concert in Lewisburg's Carnegie Hall, an imposing building donated to the town by millionaire Andrew Carnegie in 1902. The first half of the program was taken up with short solos and duets, including three of Madame's dances, 'Waterlilies', 'Farewell' and 'Christmas Song'. 'Whispers, Cries and Angels' made up the second half. With this concert, I made myself, and also Madame's style of Central European dance, known to dance lovers in Lewisburg. The reception was very warm, and my confidence began to return.

Trillium presented new dance works each year, often with guest artists from outside Lewisburg, and I saw that I could make my own contribution to these performances. I found wonderful collaborators in the dancers Beth White, Carli Maraneck, Lorrie Monte, Barry Harel, Samara Michaelson and others. Barry had a natural Bodenwieser-like style which I cultivated in her. I thought Madame would have been proud of me.

As I was receiving support for my work, I finally gained the courage to turn to past inspirations. This meant opening what I was still calling my 'India Bag' – it was now a treasure trove of memories and images from all my travels through life – and diving into the bag to find what I could use.

Back in India I had begun to think about a story for a dance drama – about the Buddha's wife and her dilemma when he went in search of enlightenment and left her with a child. I realised that this story was the one for which I'd created those large, outlandish masks of the 'caravan people' in Karachi. They were very much inspired by statues of the Buddha.

There, fully formed, I found *The Buddha's Wife* waiting for me – if only the Trillium dancers would give their time for rehearsals. I went about trying to interest them in the story and I'm glad to say I succeeded.

We began to work. I made the large masks just as I had in Karachi: the caravan people, the ladies of the bedchamber, the faces of the ego-self, the Buddha – and the Buddha's wife, a role I gave to myself. Then I made all the costumes.

Bill tolerated, in fact enjoyed, watching me make masks and costumes. He told his cousin, Sam Tuckwiller, fondly, 'Eileen's got masks in every room in the house.' One day, Sam was sitting and chatting with Bill in the breakfast room when I entered wearing a long robe of golden tissue and asked his opinion of it. Gentleman that he was, Sam did not show his surprise. He considered the garment critically and said he thought it suited the part very well – as if he knew just what a Buddha's wife would wear.

Bill liked that I had returned to dance. The common idea was that you danced on tippy toes until you were about thirty years old, and then you became a teacher or you simply put it behind you. I did not fit into that notion, and he came to admire that spirit.

Early on, when Bill introduced me to someone, he would say, 'Eileen used to be a dancer.' Now he would boast, or as close to boasting as a humble man like Bill ever could, 'Eileen is a dancer.'

It was true. Bill had felt the change in me since we had first met on Maryat's front porch. All that I had consciously and unconsciously absorbed during my travels and as a member of the Bodenwieser group had come together in this little town of Lewisburg, West Virginia, with the support of Trillium and The Dance Studio. I could see myself as a creative artist again, just as I had found peace and happiness with Bill, and he with me.

On New Year's Eve, 1997, Bill and I went driving as usual. We had dinner at a restaurant, then went home to watch television. We were waiting for the sound of fireworks and midnight celebrations, but I was concerned for

Mr Puss. He'd been missing for two days, which was not like him at all.

'I'm going to look for Mr Puss,' I told Bill. 'I'll be back soon.'

'All right,' Bill replied.

Those were the last words he ever said to me. When I returned to the television room fifteen minutes later, he was sitting in his chair as though peacefully sleeping.

I sat down for a moment then phoned Bill's son Raymond, who lived not very far away. He said to me later he had known why I had called even before I told him. He came straight away and for some time we sat together not saying anything, except that Raymond called the undertaker.

That was the end of my life with Bill, my true love.

I was consumed with sadness, but for myself, not with grief for his suffering. I had not grieved that way for Baruch, who had died full of anger. That was a very bitter sort of grief. This was sweeter, somehow, and softer.

Bill's death was peaceful. In accepting the ways of nature, Bill had accepted death, I believe, as nature's way of returning us to the source. Of course, he hadn't wanted to die, but his last days were calm and sweet.

I continued living in our house for another six months. Mr Puss had returned – who knows what adventures he had been up to. But otherwise, on my own, the fourteen rooms seemed very large, and Bill's presence was very strong. At night, as I slept upstairs, I could swear I heard footsteps creaking on the floorboards downstairs.

I lived as I had with Bill by my side – I would cook bacon and egg and grits, just as when we had dined at home. Then I would sit and watch television, not minding that I was alone, while still finding it hard to believe Bill was not alive. The mystery of being, and suddenly ceasing to be, puzzled me.

After six months, a nice, distinguished couple bought the property. Suddenly, the house was full of Bill's children and grandchildren, working at a great pace, emptying it of all its precious furniture, Chinese carpets and heirlooms. Just seven days after the sale, the new owners moved in, and Mr Puss and I moved to a small cottage on the far side of the garden that Bill and his family had purchased for me to live in should this time ever come.

In truth, I was not sure that I belonged in the Greenbrier Valley without Bill. I felt as though my home really had more to do with Bill than the country we lived on. Even as I lived amidst all that beauty – the mountain ridges, the creek, the valley – it all seemed very still and quiet as the days went by.

The nights, though. If I listened carefully, out of the stillness of the dark came a subtle symphony. A long, low hum, and then, emerging above the hum, small clicks, keens, moans – the sounds of a million tiny beings living their lives. The swish of wings, distant calls: of hello, of longing, of fear. I would keep very still as I listened. The snap of a twig could throw the whole world into silence, but I knew if I were to wait a while, the great song of life would fill the night again. Now and again a noise would draw close, and I'd try and discern the animal or insect from which the sounds came, but no creatures would appear.

One night I sat on the valley ridge with Mr Puss, wondering if he could see the mysterious creatures out in the night. He was a bright cat – as smart and loving as a dog, but without all the tail-wagging fuss and neediness with which dogs show their love.

That night, despite Mr Puss's sensible friendship, I felt my solitude keenly. As the night deepened and the glorious song of clicks and switches started up, a new sound began to swell, as if a million tiny engines were revving up, until it all came to a sudden stop and a million fireflies took to the air, transforming the valley into a great mirror of the night sky above the mountain tops. The silky black darkness was studded with moving points of light, and above, the stars opened in the sky.

It was one of the most magical moments of my life. I yearned for someone to share my rapture, and at that moment, Mr Puss looked up and our eyes met.

I'd never seen a cat look at me with such understanding.

'Isn't it marvellous? Isn't it wonderful?' his eyes said to me. 'We are in this together.'

And so we sat, woman and cat, side by side, united in connection to the great *ommmm* of the universe, while the stars danced above us, and the fireflies danced below.

Chapter Twelve

Sydney / Let's Dance

After Bill's death, I continued to work with my wonderful colleagues at Trillium, and we produced several of my dance dramas. One was particularly dear to me. The idea had begun with a poem by my friend and Bodenwieser dancer Coralie Hinkley, called 'Star', but at some point I left the words of the poem behind, and the work evolved into a kind of archetypal drama about life, death and resurrection after darkness, drawing on the ancient Egyptian story of Isis and Osiris as well as astrophysics. I called it *Osiris and the Black Hole*. We staged it at Carnegie Hall in 2003 and I dedicated the performance to Bill. His daughter Lucie and son Raymond both came to the concert and brought flowers. I think they were very pleased.

I made short trips back to Australia, including for several reunions of Bodenwieser dancers. I remember one in 2007. Coralie couldn't make it, nor could Jean Raymond, Shona Dunlop or dear Basil Pattison – which was a shame. But Moira Claux, Elaine Vallance, Anita Ardell, Eva Nadas and Biruta Apens were there. These people felt like family to me – we shared so much. We were all very excited to see each other.

Then, in 2013, I decided it was time – I needed to go home to Australia for good. I picked up the phone and booked passage on an airplane. I took only a few clothes and some costuming. I left behind the many reels of the film I'd made with Baruch, stored at the local college. I wonder whether they are still there.

I wanted to see a gum tree. I wanted to wake up each morning and hear a kookaburra. I'm not sure why the sound of a kookaburra touches me so deeply. It's part of my childhood. But it's also, I don't know, so flagrantly joyous.

Not long after landing in Sydney, I was walking in Double Bay, and just as I passed a woman walking the other way, a kookaburra burst into song above us.

'Oh!' I cried out. 'I travelled across the whole world to hear that sound!'

'Oh!' the lady cried right back. 'Did-ja? Did-ja, darlin'?'

She had the most wonderfully Australian manner and I thought, *Well! I'm back!*

When I first arrived, I stayed with my friend Barbara Cuckson in Paddington. I'd known Barbara her whole life – she had been in one of Madame's children's classes. She was very kind and patient, but when she'd had enough of me, she told me quite frankly that I could not stay with her forever. She said I should call something called ACAT, which I later discovered stands for 'Aged Care Assessment Team'. Had I known that, I wouldn't have had anything to do with them. I thought they were arranging cat adoptions or something like that; I am quite fond of cats, you know.

Well, two women from ACAT came and Barbara offered them afternoon tea, which they politely declined. We discussed how much money I had brought with me from America. I thought it was quite a bit, but apparently not. It seemed I was at risk of becoming homeless. They got out their iPads and did some thinking and talking and typing and then said they would come back to take me to a place called 'Thurles Castle' in Chippendale.

The next day they returned and bundled me into a car with my luggage and some things Barbara thought at the last minute I might need, like a cushion and some forks and spoons, and we set off for my new home.

'Chippendale!' I was thinking. 'Who lives in Chippendale?'

But Chippendale had changed since I was young, and I liked what I found when we got there. Thurles Castle had once been a pub. It was built around a lovely, sunny courtyard, in which I met eight or so people who were to become my friends. It was a cosmopolitan group. There was Peter the Greek, who would hose down the garden against the heat; Old Mr Reuben, a sophisticated, intellectual, elderly Jewish man who could somehow balance eight cups of tea and coffee all the way from the kitchen to our little social group in the courtyard; and William Murray, who until recently had been a professor of English in China – he would help me later when I let it be known I was working on a book.

Once I'd settled in, I became very comfortable at Thurles Castle. The building was on a corner, but the cross street was closed off so there was no through traffic, and right opposite was Brickfields bakery and cafe. All I had to do was open the big doors and stroll out to get a coffee and sit for a while. It was a lovely spot – with nice benches and a couple of palm trees to lend their shade. I liked to observe the people around me – students from the university and their professors – a lovely atmosphere that reminded me of New York.

I went to Brickfields every morning and after a while I said to the young man who ran it, 'What's been going on? I've been away for 60 years, and I've come back to find a country covered with squashed avocados.'

The young man's name was Lacey Cole. He was also a musician, and we got on very well. About six months after I arrived in Australia, it was my hundredth birthday, and Brickfields held a lovely street party for me, with a special, giant cake.

To repay Lacey's kindness, I performed in a film clip for his song 'Nephilim's Lament', on the windswept rocks at the end of Clovelly Beach. I was pleased with the result, although I must say it wasn't easy to dance on those rocks – all the little periwinkle shells were a nuisance on the feet.

I was starting to think I'd better get moving with the next phase of my life.

I also missed Madame very much. I knew she had died but she had always seemed so indestructible. Now I was back in Australia I somehow expected her to be here too.

One day I was having coffee at Brickfields and I noticed a young woman looking closely at me. Eventually she came over and sat down next to me, and we struck up a conversation. Her name was Shane Carroll. She was a dancer, she said.

'I am a dancer too,' I told her. 'I was a member of the first modern dance company in New South Wales.'

'The Bodenwieser dancers?' said Shane.

Oh, thank goodness, I thought. *How wonderful! Madame is not forgotten altogether.*

It was wonderful enough that Shane knew about Madame; what happened next was perhaps even more wonderful; one might even say life-changing.

Shane went and told Dr Maggie Haertsch about me. Maggie was running an organisation called the Arts Health Institute, and she was interested in experienced artists who had been around a long time and were still creating.

That sounded just like me, so Shane introduced me to Maggie, who took us all out for high tea at a little hotel in Woollahra. I was terribly impressed. She was so 'with it' and well dressed. We got along wonderfully, and after that Maggie took me in hand. Some new residents had moved into Thurles Castle and the atmosphere had changed. So I went to live near her, in a street lined with terrace houses, until finally she found me a place in the rather grand sandstone retirement home where I now live.

This was very good of her. It is always nice to have a 'home', although I had no interest in the 'retirement' part of it. I never say I am retired because I am not.

Nonetheless, I like it here. I have a room of my own, and in the peaceful hours I think and work.

Maggie made me an ambassador for the Arts Health Institute. Through her, I began to meet all sorts of people, from politicians to businessmen, fashion designers and artists. She took me to Uluru – an extraordinary experience. She arranged publicity campaigns to raise money when I started to make dance works so we could pay people and buy materials.

Amazingly enough, there seemed to be a lot of interest in me and what I was doing. I did television talk shows, photoshoots and radio interviews; the ABC made a documentary for its *Compass* program, which led to a friendship with producer Tracey Spring, and that in turn led to us working together on a book of stories about my life in Sydney in the 1930s: *Eileen: Stories from the Phillip Street Courtyard*. I went to the Gold Coast with Tracey for a role in an episode of the TV series *The End*, with Frances O'Connor. I had a part in a rather odd production of *The Wizard of Oz* at the Belvoir Street Theatre, and through that, met the talented Paul Capsis, who remains a friend. Fashion designer Brigid McLaughlin made my drawings into beautiful scarves that she sold in her shop; she too became a friend. It was like a wave, one thing led to another and yet another. Very exciting.

Shane also brought me together with choreographer and filmmaker Sue Healey. Shane told me Sue was someone I really should meet, and she was not wrong. It was clear to me that Sue was an impressive contemporary dancer and creative choreographer. Her work had people leaping about in street clothes in underground caverns. Lots of fast movement and high kicks. Not very Bodenwieser-like. But she was very curious about Bodenwieser, and about the fact that I was still dancing after so many years.

We found each other very interesting. What soon struck me about Sue, was that although our dance styles are a bit different, we shared the same feeling or instinct for stillness. As we got to know each other, I realised there was a great deal I could learn from her, and she from me. She has created several video portraits of me, one of which is in the National Portrait Gallery in Canberra – I do like the idea of a portrait that moves. And together we have made three short films – a trilogy. I am very proud of all of them. The most recent, *Waterlily Variations*, is a tribute to Madame.

At the core of all this work are the wonderful performers and my dear friends: Anca Frankenhaeuser, Patrick Harding-Irmer, Julia Cotton, the indispensable Geoff Weston. And Sue and Shane, of course.

Ever since that fateful moment when I met Shane in Brickfields cafe, and she introduced me to Maggie and Sue, it has felt like the best years of my life were unfolding. Even when the COVID pandemic came along in 2020 and we were told to stay inside, this blossoming continued.

Yes, it was inconvenient; it changed the way I worked with other people. My trusty phone became even more important than usual – and I discovered the lovely 'Siri'. But in the scheme of things, I didn't mind the isolation one bit. I never felt lonely or confined. I had my ideas, my writing and my drawing to keep me company. As long as you have a pen in your hand, you are never lonely.

I've always liked to draw. When you draw, something is guiding the movement you make with your hand. It's you, of course, but maybe more than you as well. To make big sweeps, bold moves – and also small, subtle, intricate ones – with a pen or a pencil requires the same commitment as making a dance move. A drawing is a kind of dance on paper, one that lasts forever.

Through drawings and sketches, I explore ideas and keep track of my projects as they evolve. I had loved making the illustrations for the book of stories from my Phillip Street days. And during the lockdown, drawings helped me convey my thoughts to Sue as she edited the film we had just finished shooting before COVID arrived.

Lockdown was also the perfect time to write another book. A lovely gentleman here where I live had offered to read to me in the evenings. Then I befriended his daughter, Cathy Gray, a writer and editor, who volunteered to transcribe some stories I was writing, and, as we've gotten closer, these began to turn into something interesting. I opened up my India Bag again (an increasingly inaccurate term for all the treasures from around the world in there!) and as I went through my memories, I found they became joined in different ways; this recollection attached to that image, to a flight of fancy, to a philosophical moment. Cathy helped me find what was special about each story, and we published the best of them in a collection named *Elephants and Other Stories*. She has been a wonderful editor to work with. Like Maryat, she understands the value of following a vision. She would never tell me to cut out the magical parts of a story! They are the best bits – just like in life.

In November 2020, I was still in lockdown, but my friends surprised me with a party for my 106th birthday. I was delighted – and very touched. While I couldn't join them, the staff here where I live fixed a chair inside the bay window and gave me balloons to shake. Outside, my friends danced for me – to Louis Armstrong's 'Kiss of Fire'.

There have been two more birthdays since then, and I have found myself treated to new 'Kiss of Fire' choreography each time. My endlessly inventive friends.

※

I cannot tell you how wonderful it is to find like-minded people to help me to continue to bring my visions to life – on the page, through drawing, through dance.

Sometimes, when it is quiet, I will think of a friend and realise that they are gone. At a certain point, if you live as long as I have, you realise that so many of the friends you have made are dead. Most recently, Coralie Hinkley, who died in November 2021. I can't quite believe Coralie is no more. She was such a strong dancer.

It's a sad thought, but I am so fortunate to find myself surrounded by new friends and artists who inspire me to keep working. When I first came back to Sydney, I felt I would sit on the beach and do nothing. Perhaps get a sunburn, nothing more. But I have been too busy! Since I've come back, I've created two live dance dramas and three dance films, led two workshops at dance festivals, been in a TV series, a stage show and three music videos, and published two books. Life keeps me dancing.

I'm so glad I came back here. I have some wonderful friends. I'm still dancing in the style of Bodenwieser. Most importantly, I have been having a marvellous time. I think that's important to remember – that at 108, you can have a great time, doing new work. And you never stop learning.

༄

We live in an age of science, and I feel excited when I learn about new scientific developments. I heard the other day that scientists have discovered that trees talk to each other over vast distances, using a secret language of underground fungus. Can you imagine? The secrets they must keep!

People are always talking about God and his people, as though humans are the most special creations. But how can we be, in a world where trees talk with one another?

I feel like the trees, the animals, know themselves better than we do. I think humans still have a long way to go.

I don't believe there is such a thing as death – what we call death is simply our fabric taking on a new shape. You go on to a new shape, a new planet, and gradually you learn the steps and lessons of that life. And by the time you have been all the way around the universe, and lived on all the different planets, you will have taken every shape the universe has in store for you. After all that, I like to think we become a creature of pure spirit, the one we can only glimpse in ecstatic moments of this life. Because who wants to be human forever? A human is not the most remarkable shape to be, compared to some of what is out there.

I've been here for 108 years. It may be nearly time I left, go on to the next planet, started the next journey. I don't want to leave; I still like it here. But I'm not worried about death.

Now and again, all through my life, people have told me, 'I wish I could do what you have done. I could never do that.'

To which I say, 'Yes, you could! What is stopping you? Your career? Your job? Do you want to be a hundred years old and look back at your life and know that you never did the crazy thing your heart told you to do?'

I have had many adventures, created many things. On the way I have made many mistakes. But I have few regrets.

All I am certain about is that I have learned a lot on my journey through this world. And that I had the great luck, and joy, to be a student of Madame's.

My only wish is that people I loved along the way could be here. Richard, Baruch, Bill, Roie, Evelyn,

Bettina, my beloved Emmy. And Madame herself. It is a small wish, but I would like the chance to tell them one thing. The same thing that I would like to tell you. That from the day I first truly became alive, up until today, I would like them to know that I was, and remain, a Bodenwieser dancer.

What the next steps on the journey will be, I don't know, but I intend to dance them with all the feeling and passion that Madame bequeathed to me. These gifts have been my companions through the years. Life has kept me dancing, and the dance will go on. Thank you for being my partner as I have danced through my memories. I hope you will think of me next time you hear music that inspires you to move, and think of me as I am now, sitting in front of my lovely mirror, in this lovely body, asking the woman in front of me: 'Shall we dance?'

Acknowledgements

When the lovely Cate Blake got in touch after my 108th birthday last year with the idea of doing a book with Pan Macmillan, my first thought was . . . *goodness, do I have time?*

Yes, it has been a busy six months, but it has also been very rewarding. Cate introduced me to novelist Liam Pieper, and through our conversations over many weeks Liam was able to tease out skeins of memories, reflections on memories – and new insights into things I thought I had forgotten – that have become the warp and weft of this book. I thank both Cate and Liam for their sensitivity and enthusiasm, as well as their craft.

We have also drawn on my previous memoir, *Walkabout Dancer*, self-published in 2008 while I was living in West Virginia, as well as some of the stories from the book I did with Tracey Spring in 2018, published by

Melbourne Books: *Eileen, Stories from the Phillip Street Courtyard*, and from my 2021 self-published collection *Elephants and Other Stories*. All of these are still available online if you would like to explore my adventures a bit further.

I initially wanted to call this book 'Not all about me', but in her publisher's wisdom, Cate didn't think that quite worked. It is about me, of course. But in being about 'me', it is also about a great many others, whom I would like to acknowledge here.

Firstly, for everything that is good about my current life in Sydney, I want to express my very deep gratitude to Shane Carroll, Maggie Haertsch, and my wonderful collaborator and soulmate Sue Healey.

Then there are the talented dancers who, along with Shane and Sue, continue to help me realise my projects in Sydney: Anca Frankenhaeuser, Patrick Harding-Irmer, Julia Cotton – all of them dear friends; as well as the beautiful young dancers Lucy Gold, Allie Graham, Renata Commisso and Kei Ikeda. And other collaborators of all kinds: composers Mike Nock, Laurence Pike and Ben Walsh; cinematographers Richard Corfield and Mark Pugh.

Deepest thanks also to the friends and supporters who enhance my days in so many practical ways through their care and comradeship: Geoff Weston, Francoise

Fombertaux and Paul Orchard, Kylie Washington-Smith, Brigid McLaughlin, Paul Capsis, Tobi Wilkinson and Rob Keldoulis (aka The Husband), Sue Burrows.

More broadly, thank you to the many people everywhere who have helped fund my projects and followed my work over the years.

I also want to acknowledge Barbara Cuckson, for her ongoing stewardship of the Bodenwieser archives held by the National Library of Australia. She is my go-to person for checking all things Bodenwieser, and a dear friend as well.

And a shout-out across the world to my friends and collaborators from the Trillium Performing Arts Collective in Lewisburg, West Virginia: Carli Mareneck, Beth White, Lorrie Monte, Barry Harel, Samara Michaelson, Jo Weisbrod – in many ways I found myself again creatively through my work with you.

Closer to home, I must mention the management and staff of Lulworth House, who look after me so well, and put up with me cluttering my room with half-made costumes and masks and piles of paper.

Finally, to my friend Cathy Gray, thank you for believing in this project and being there every step of the way. I couldn't have done it without you.

Eileen Kramer
June 2023